Joseph Addison

Twayne's English Authors Series

Bertram H. Davis, Editor

Florida State University

TEAS 338

Portrait by Sir Godfrey Kneller
Courtesy of National Portrait Gallery, London

Joseph Addison

By Robert M. Otten

Saint Anselm College

Twayne Publishers • *Boston*

Joseph Addison

Robert M. Otten

Copyright © 1982 by G. K. Hall & Company
All Rights Reserved
Published by Twayne Publishers
A Division of G. K. Hall & Company
70 Lincoln Street
Boston, Massachusetts 02111

Book production by Marne B. Sultz
Book design by Barbara Anderson

Printed on permanent/durable acid-free
paper and bound in The United States
of America.

Library of Congress Cataloging in Publication Data

Otten, Robert M.
  Joseph Addison.

(Twayne's English authors series; TEAS 338)
Bibliography: p. 172
Includes index.
1. Addison, Joseph, 1672–1719—Criticism and inter-
pretation. I. Title. II. Series.
PR3307.08   1982   824'.5   82–1087
ISBN 0–8057–6824–6   AACR2

To Betsy

Contents

About the Author

Robert M. Otten is associate professor of English at Saint Anselm College, where he teaches courses in composition, eighteenth-century and twentieth-century English literature, and Russian literature. He received the B.A. from St. John's University and the Ph.D. from the University of Notre Dame; he has done postdoctoral work at Smith College and the University of North Carolina. He is currently at work on a study of Lancelot Addison, Joseph Addison's father.

Preface

A book about Addison should begin, like one of his essays, with a motto. Richmond P. Bond's comment that "Addison was not always a Secretary or a Cato or a Spectator" announces the theme of this study.

Many excellent accounts of Addison already exist. Some are biographical studies which trace the simultaneous progression of his literary and political careers. Others are critical analyses of his major writings, the tragedy *Cato* and the periodical essays in the *Tatler* and the *Spectator*. The biographical and critical accounts have a common denominator: they consider the ideas and the methods of his works between 1710 and 1714 the quintessential Addison. In a way they are right to do so, for these four years saw Addison's most concentrated imaginative achievement.

But in another way the concentration upon *Cato* and the periodical essays gives a distorted view. Addison's literary career spanned twenty-three years. He wrote English and Latin poetry, political pamphlets, a travel book, a study of Roman coins, an opera, and a comedy in addition to his most famous works. This book aims to provide a survey of Addison's entire corpus, a survey usually obtainable only by extensive reading in numerous books and articles. Even then, the student of Addison finds most of the writing treated as prologue or epilogue to *Cato* and the *Spectator*. At least once the early and the late works deserve an individual treatment.

Writers of prefaces often claim to discern a revival of interest in their author. No Addison boom hovers, at this moment, on the horizon. In their reaction against the Victorians' adulation of Addison, twentieth-century critics have pushed too much of his work out their conscious minds. Perhaps a reassessment will jog a few memories.

Robert M. Otten

Saint Anselm College

Chronology

1672   Joseph Addison born May 1, 1672, at Milston in Wiltshire, son of Lancelot Addison and Jane Gulston Addison.

1686   Attends Charterhouse School, where he meets Richard Steele.

1687   Enters Queen's College, Oxford.

1688   James II abdicates; William of Orange lands in England and claims the crown.

1689   Elected Demy at Magdalen College reputedly on the merit of his Latin verse.

1693   Takes the M.A.; publishes "To Mr. Dryden" in *Miscellany Poems*.

1694   Publishes original English poems and translations in Tonson's *Miscellany*.

1695   Publishes a "Poem to His Majesty."

1697   Publishes "Pax Gulielmi"; his "Essay on Vergil's *Georgics*" printed as introduction to Dryden's translation.

1698   Becomes a Fellow of Magdalen College.

1699   Edits second volume of *Musarum Anglicanarum Analecta*, containing seven of his Latin poems. Receives a pension of £200 to travel on the Continent. Arrives at Paris in December.

1700   Studies the French language at Paris and Blois; begins tour of Italy.

1702   Tours Switzerland, Germany, Austria, and Holland; death of King William ends his pension; Princess Anne becomes queen.

1704   Elected to the Kit-Kat Club; writes "The Campaign" at the behest of Godolphin and Halifax to celebrate Marlborough's victory at Blenheim; appointed Commissioner of Appeals as a reward.

1705   Publishes *Remarks Upon Italy* and helps Steele revise his comedy *The Tender Husband;* accompanies Lord Halifax on a diplomatic mission to Hanover.

1706   Appointed Undersecretary of State first to Sir Charles Hedges and then to the Earl of Sunderland.

1707   His opera *Rosamond* runs three nights; enters the world of partisan pamphleteering with "The Present State of the War."

1708   Elected to Parliament for Lostwiethel; appointed chief secretary to the Earl of Wharton, Lord Lieutenant of Ireland.

1709   First contribution to the *Tatler,* part of No. 18; in late November begins frequent contributions.

1710   Frequent contributions to the *Tatler* in spring and fall; in late summer and fall publishes five numbers of *Whig Examiner* in defense of Whig administration; elected to Parliament for Malmsbury.

1711   On March 1 begins regular publication of the *Spectator* with Steele; purchases an estate at Bilton Hall.

1713   Sees *Cato* run for twenty-five nights; publishes the "Tryal of Count Tariff" and contributes fifty-one numbers to Steele's *Guardian.* Presides over the "Little Senate" at Button's Coffee-House.

1714   In June revives the *Spectator* with assistance of Eustace Budgell; after Queen Anne dies, appointed secretary to the Lord Justices and Regency during accession of George of Hanover to the English throne.

1715   Appointed Commissioner of Trade; begins *The Freeholder* in defense of George I when the Pretender, James III, invades Ireland.

1716   *The Drummer* runs three nights in March. In August marries the Countess of Warwick.

1717   Serves as Secretary of State.

1718   Resigns as Secretary of State because of ill health.

1719   His daughter Charlotte born; publishes *The Old Whig*, defending the Peerage Bill, against Steele's *The Plebeian*. Dies on June 17.

1721   First collected edition of Addison's works published by Thomas Tickell.

Chapter One
Politician and Poet

Some say that political administration was Joseph Addison's vocation and that literature was his avocation. Others claim that government service was the avocation and writing the vocation. Like most disputed cases, this one has right on both sides. For Joseph Addison service to the government of England and a literary career were the halves of one scheme of life. Only the fortunes of the Whig party in the reigns of King William, Queen Anne, and George I decided which component was vocation and which was avocation at any given moment. Sometimes the twin purposes were indistinguishably one when the subject of writing was a political crisis or principle.

Because Addison's literary works are so entwined with his political career, his writings can never be separated from the context of events in England during his lifetime. English political, intellectual and literary life underwent revolutions between 1675 and 1725. Sometimes these revolutions influenced one another; at other times they simply coincided. Thus the changes that occurred in these fifty years are not easy for the modern reader to sort out or keep track of. But an understanding of the general shift in politics, learning and literature is essential to an appreciation of the ideas which recur in Addison's writings and the changing modes of expression in which they appear.

A Revolutionary Age

Joseph Addison's life (1672–1719) coincides with a revolutionary period in English history. Both at home and abroad the country underwent important shifts in power: Parliament contested the monarchy for an equal share in governing the land,

and Britain contested France for the commercial and political
leadership of Europe. Simultaneously, many thinkers began to
revise the way men looked upon their world and themselves: the
new philosophy, as it was called, challenged the supremacy of
Aristotelian physics in understanding the universe and the necessity of Christian doctrine in understanding society and human
nature. And, finally, a generation of writers—Steele, Swift, Addison, and others—involved literature in the political and intellectual revolutions to the exclusion of most other subjects and
made English prose the literary equal of poetry.

The domestic political situation of the last quarter of the seventeenth century is fundamental because it dictated the kind of
writer Addison became. Out of disagreements in Parliament over
the policies of King Charles II and the possible succession of the
Catholic James II rose two contending political groups, the Tories
and the Whigs—each group named contemptuously by its opponents. Those who favored a strong royal government and op-
posed religious toleration for Protestants who did not conform
to the doctrines or beliefs of the Anglican Church were called
"Tories" (a name for Irish Catholic bandits) by their opponents;
those who wished to limit royal authority and preferred a national
church with a broad enough ritual and doctrine to encompass all
Protestants were called "Whigs" (a name for Scottish Presbyterian
rebels) by their opponents.[1] These names stuck, although in the
coming years new issues and conflicts would alter the principles
for which the two parties stood.

Although contending parties for power were nothing new in
England, there was a new factor in political warfare. Contention
was legal, not treasonous. Whigs and Tories contended for the
power that Parliamentary majorities and ministerial posts brought.
Two factors insured that such contests would be hotly fought.
An enlarged franchise and frequent elections after the Triennial
Act of 1694 meant that more voters had to be persuaded more
often.[2] And the precarious constitutional position of the three
monarchs who succeeded James II insured that no ruler could rely
upon either Whigs or Tories exclusively. Both situations demanded that the political parties add public relations to their bag

of political tricks. Public relations demanded persuasive writers. Anyone who could write well—and many who could not—were swept up naturally in or recruited deliberately for the political controversy that marks the reigns of William III (1698–1702), Anne (1702–1714), and George I (1714–1727).

William of Orange, leader of the Dutch Republic, did not come to the English throne in the normal course of hereditary succession, but because his father-in-law, James II, alienated most of his Protestant subjects by his efforts to strengthen the royal power and restore Catholicism. Invited by a number of English leaders, William landed in England in November 1688 with a Dutch army, presumably to defend the right of his wife, Mary, to the English crown. When James II conveniently fled to France, William insisted upon a share of the royal power; he and Mary were crowned joint rulers in February 1689. His crown never sat securely: the differences between Whigs and Tories made it difficult for him to find ministers in either party who would support his policies and who could also obtain broad public support. Some Englishmen, predominantly Tory in outlook, refused to accept the settlement which gave him the crown, and Englishmen of both parties had little real enthusiasm for a foreign king who seemed to trust his Dutch advisors more than his new subjects. In foreign affairs William reversed a long tradition of cooperation with France. Since 1672, as leader of the Dutch, William had formed alliances and waged war against the domination of Europe by France. When he became king of England, he engaged England in that war, which continued until 1697. When it appeared in 1700 that Louis XIV might establish dynastic control over the Spanish empire, William formed another alliance to resist this accession of power to the "Sun King." The war which resulted, the War of the Spanish Succession, was breaking out when William died in 1702.

Anne was much more beloved than William: she was English in upbringing, and in direct succession to James II and her older sister Mary, who had died in 1694. But during her reign Whigs and Tories fought continuously for control of Parliament and the ministry. For most of her reign Anne aimed at a compromise government. The major issue was the War of the Spanish Succession. The Tories generally recommended a moderate policy toward France and Spain. The Whigs generally pursued a harsher policy: no peace until France was defeated, and an all-out land war on the Continent to break the might of Louis XIV's armies. Other issues complicated English politics. The Tories felt that concessions to Dissenters threatened the position of the established Church, while Whigs fought to protect the limited toleration which had been given to non-Anglican Protestants. The Whig ministers who led the war raised large loans from London financiers, and helped pay for the war by a land tax which fell heavily upon Tory landed gentlemen. When the Whigs overreached themselves by putting on trial a Tory preacher, Queen Anne turned to the Tories in 1710. Bitter partisan conflict continued on the heated issues of the terms of peace with France, the rights of the Church and the Dissenters, and the succession to the throne.

Queen Anne died in 1714, leaving no direct heir. In 1701 a Tory-dominated Parliament had passed the Act of Settlement, which stated that the rulers of the House of Hanover in Germany were next in line for the crown. After Anne's death George, Elector of Hanover, became king of England as George I. His assumption of the throne took place peaceably, although there were fears of plots to restore the son of James II. A rebellion in Scotland in 1715 in favor of the Stuart claimant was easily suppressed. Once again England accepted a foreign ruler, this time a German prince who did not speak the English language, who retained a strong interest in Hanover and its place among the German states, and who brought with him a group of Hanoverian advisers and mistresses who excited envy and contempt. Because many Tories seemed willing to welcome back a Stuart king, George turned to the Whigs for support, and an election in 1715 gave his Whig ministers a strong majority in the House of Commons. George I was accepted because the English people wanted to support the Protestant succession, as determined in the Act of Settlement, and wanted security and stability instead of the foreign and domestic strife which had been their lot since the Revolution of 1688–89.

An intellectual revolution accompanied the political. It was in fact the last stage of a change in thought underway throughout the seventeenth century as the "New Science" of Copernicus, Descartes, and Bacon replaced the theories of Ptolme, Aristotle, and other classical authorities. This last stage, a noisy and emblematic pamphlet war waged by a handful of writers and gentleman-scholars, is known as the Controversy of the Ancients and the Moderns. The dispute turned on whether intellectual life ought to be spent in imitation of the philosophy and learning inherited from Greece and Rome or whether intellectual life ought to blaze its own paths. The party of the Ancients asserted that men could only hope to emulate the achievements of the past. The party of the Moderns replied that men knew more already than the past had bequeathed and possessed the tools, especially the experimental method of Francis Bacon, to learn even more. The quarrelers usually pitted the literary and ethical genius of classical writers against the technological and scientific progress of the moderns. The controversy began in France and came to England through Sir William Temple's essay "Of Ancient and Modern Learning." Temple sided with the Ancients, but his essay provoked a literary warfare between supporters and detractors in the 1690s and early 1700s.

But if ancient philosophy had to contend against modern science, classical historians, poets and moralists still had their use. The works of the Greek and Roman writers could provide a way of understanding the upheavals and tensions of the modern, changing world:

Classicists of the late seventeenth and early eighteenth centuries used classical literature to throw their own age into perspective, to light its outstanding qualities so they could be objectively examined. They used that literature to get at the inner meaning of daily affairs, a meaning that would otherwise be revealed only by time. They used it as a standard of achievement, a model and a warning the more effective for being remote, whole and exhaustive. Classicism was not a monolithic penchant for literary imitation, but a rationale for life.[3]

There was also another advantage of classicism: it was secular. Many wished to see eliminated the religious factionalism which was thought to have caused rebellion and bloodshed in the past; the ancient writers provided an alternative to the Bible as the place in which to read a commentary on the present. Likewise many wished to see the state freed of its partnership with the church; Augustan Rome demonstrated a period in which artists and not priests took the role of educating the citizenry.

Inevitably, these changes in politics and learning led to changes in literature.[4] In the seventeenth century writers were essentially amateurs; usually they were aristocrats or clergymen, those who possessed the education and leisure to pursue literary interests. Their works circulated in manuscript within a select and interested group; publishing for a wide audience was secondary. Dramatic literature likewise existed for a small audience of kings and courtiers who supported acting companies, patronized the few theaters, and watched their values and frolics portrayed upon the stage. But by the early eighteenth century authorship became a profession. Publication brought literary recognition and profit if a writer could interest a large audience in his wares. The medium of expression changed as authorship did. In the 1600s poetry was the primary language. Literary criticism, philosophy, and political theory—as well as personal experience—were regularly cast in verse. By the time Addison died, English prose had supplanted verse as the predominent literary mode. Prose now not only communicated information on every subject but did so with artistry.

The changes in authorship and expression rested partly on the change in reading public. Men of business and ladies enlarged a readership previously composed of clergymen and aristocrats. The interest of these readers demanded attention as well. To the discussion of religion and political issues were added topics of daily interest: the manners and mores of polite society, virtues and attitudes appropriate to a nation claiming international leadership, scientific discoveries made by the new philosophy, and trends in the arts.

Not in His Father's Steps

One can appreciate the effect of these changes by comparing Joseph Addison's career and attitudes with those of his father Lancelot Addison. Joseph Addison began his education with the probable intention of becoming, like his father, a priest of the established Church. Since Lancelot Addison could not afford to give his son much of an estate, Joseph would have to make his own way in the world. In 1687 Joseph started in his father's footsteps by enrolling at Queen's College, Oxford, Lancelot's alma mater.

Lancelot Addison's life had been what Joseph could look forward to. Lancelot began his clerical career as a chaplain to the commander of the British bases at Dunkirk and Tangier. After several years abroad he settled with Jane Gulston in the village of Milston in Wiltshire, where Joseph was born May 1, 1672. A learned man, Lancelot Addison did not let his education go to waste. He published several books on the Mohammedan culture he had seen at Tangier. When a debate developed in 1680 on the wisdom of retaining the Tangier base, Lancelot committed himself to the fray by publishing a pamphlet urging that it be kept. He took his religious duties seriously as well, publishing a spirited defense of his profession during the anticlerical days of the 1670s as well as a call to the Church to take its teaching duties seriously. Lancelot Addison, a pious man, composed a book of devotional poems which reflect his love of church ritual and his living faith. Like John Donne's holy sonnets—but scarcely as literary—his poems dramatize the Christian experience of sin, repentance, and reconciliation.

Lancelot Addison's works reveal a seventeenth-century orthodox mentality. Any religious question—whether raised in argument with Protestant dissenters, Catholics, or Mohammedans—was settled by appeal to Scripture. Political principle and social custom as well as doctrinal point were best proved by citing chapter and verse. The history of Morocco which chaplain Lancelot had learned firsthand was not just interesting reading but a commentary upon God's plan for England. As Addison read Moslem history, Mohammed carved a new religion out of his own fanatical ideas and propagated it by the sword. It was an emblem of what had gone wrong in England in the 1640s: the Puritan zealots, unchecked in time by the power of the king or the established church, had overthrown divinely appointed government and plunged England into civil war. Domestic and foreign history alike, warned Lancelot Addison, proved that nothing should upset the Providential plan for England: a strong Stuart monarchy ruling by God's grace in partnership with the Anglican Church.

The revolution of 1688 did not fit into the scheme of things. When the Anglican hierarchy convened in 1689 to face the new political order, Lancelot could not accept all the changes. When King William asked for reform to bring dissenting sects into the established Church, Lancelot was among those who resisted such change. His modestly successful career, which had moved him from the parish at Milston to the deanery at Lichfield, came to a halt. He was no longer in step with the times.

Joseph Addison, on the other hand, was in step. He enthusiastically hailed the coming of William and Mary; his first published work, a Latin poem printed in an Oxford University anthology celebrating the new royal couple, portrayed the dawn of a golden age. When King William's army defeated James II's forces at the Battle of the Boyne, Addison contributed a Latin poem to a second anthology. His commitment to the new rulers was poetic and wholehearted.

But the difference between Joseph and his father was more fundamental. Joseph Addison caught the excitement for both classical learning and the new philosophy. Indicative of his interests are the two Latin prose pieces he did at Oxford. One surveys the best Latin poets, especially those of Rome's Augustan age. The second argues on behalf of the new philosophy against the old. His ringing conclusion dismisses all thinkers who slavishly followed Aristotelian philosophy: "Let us therefore sentence forever this troop of commentators, to be tied up in chains and libraries, food only for moths and worms, and there let them quietly grow old, free from the sight of any reader."[5]

In his writing Addison seldom appeals to scripture as the authority for political principles, social institutions, or ethical conduct. Even for his religious ideas he prefers to rest his understanding on other sources. For instance, his last literary project was an essay "Of the Christian Religion" which sought to establish faith on reasonable grounds: he begins the search by considering "what undoubted authorities are extant among Pagan writers" (407). When Addison wishes to praise the Creator, he often praises Him as the maker of the universe revealed by the microscope and the telescope.

But no son can totally overturn the ways of the father. Joseph Addison inherited his father's dedication to instruction. Like Lancelot, Joseph Addison would use his pen with equal skill to intervene on a political issue or to offer advice about what to believe in and how to act. His father's interest in catechetics finds its echo in Joseph's *Spectator* and *Guardian* papers, which commend with equivalent force religious belief, social behavior, and literary taste. His essays form a lay catechism for polite society. As a nineteenth century English critic noted, Addison is "the first of our lay preachers."[6]

Instead of the Anglican Church, Addison chose state service as the means to benefit mankind. It is unclear whether he lacked the piety of his father or wished to find an alternative to a Church about whose status Englishmen had squabbled for a century and a half. Whatever the reason he did not take holy orders. He found an alternative in the writers of ancient Rome, public-spirited men who devoted their lives and talents to securing a peaceful state and to building a civilization upon that peace. Addison's most recent and sensitive biographer had described the rationale of Addison's secular vocation:

It was the Roman concept of citizenship which had already impressed itself deeply upon Addison's mind. An upright character and conduct, good service to the state, with embellishments of learning, culture, and urbanity, reveal themselves as parts in a single pattern of life. The concept was that of a virtuous layman, not of a pious priest; and it afforded full scope for the political ambition which fired him from his earliest days at Oxford.[7]

Politics and Poetry

In the 1690s, Addison decided that the Whig party was the party sympathetic to the new secular philosophy and to the establishment of a strong Protestant England. It was the party through which he would pursue public service. In seven years at Oxford Addison acquired a considerable knowledge of classical culture and practiced literary skills. In 1695 and 1697 he put these talents to work in the glorification of nation, monarch, and ministers. He dedicated first a poem on King William's victory at Namur to John Somers, prominent Whig and keeper of the seal; two years later he dedicated a poem on the peace treaty of Ryswick to Charles Montagu, the Whig treasurer. Both men were noted for their patronage to artists and scientists; both men also knew the value of a skilled writer in persuading an electorate or a king.[8]

Addison won tangible admiration from Somers and Montague: a chance to keep his Oxford fellowship without taking holy orders, and a government pension to support four years of travel on the continent. Addison's tour was not a vacation. Like young men of every country preparing for state service, Addison traveled to study the language, institutions, and character of the nations which, in the shifting loyalties of European politics, could be one day allies and the next day enemies.[9]

Likewise in 1704 and 1716 Addison's literary skill won him other preferments. "The Campaign," memorializing Marlborough's victory at Blenheim, earned his first government position, as commissioner of excise appeals. *The Freeholder,* written to support George I during the Jacobite rebellion, secured him the post of a commissioner of trade. Though awarded for literary skill, these posts did demand administrative talent. Addison progressed from an undersecretaryship in 1705 to become secretary of state in 1717 because he was a capable as well as dedicated administrator.

His commitment to Whig principles and his employment in Whig ministries demanded his literary skills in times of crisis: a pamphlet in 1708 to support the Whig war policy, a periodical paper in 1710 for election propaganda, another pamphlet in 1713 to proclaim a Parliamentary victory, another periodical paper in

1719 to support the Peerage Bill. But politics also had a less direct but more influential effect on Addison's literary career. It expanded his literary horizons. In the Kit-Kat Club, a political and literary society founded by John Somers and the publisher Jacob Tonson, Whig politicians and Whig writers joined forces. Addison was only one of many writers who served their party with their pens and occasionally earned an office. When politics was not their topic, the Kit-Kat writers argued poetic principles, planned literary projects and helped one another's careers. Addison realized publicity and publishing opportunities from these associates. In 1704 Steele primed the public's interest in "The Campaign" by announcing that Addison was at work on a poem for Marlborough. In 1705 he found a publisher for a book of observations made on his tour. Two years later the *Muse's Mercury* published Addison's translation of a Horatian ode and puffed his opera *Rosamond* with a favorable review.

Rosamond indicates a new direction in Addison's literary career, the theater. *Rosamond* was a part of a Kit-Kat project to promote opera in the London theater. Two years earlier Addison had written several scenes for Steele's *The Tender Husband*, a sentimental comedy. In 1706 he wrote an epilogue for Lansdown's *The British Enchanters* and in 1708 a prologue for Smith's *Phaedra* and *Hippolytus*. Later Addison's *Cato* and *The Drummer* would be produced largely through the efforts of fellow Kit-Kat writers.

Addison discovered another genre through a Kit-Kat friend, Richard Steele. This genre of periodical journalism proved the most fertile soil for Addison's literary talents. The *Tatler* and *Spectator* essays of 1711–1713 are unlike the ones Addison wrote earlier, but they are his most perfect pieces. In the prose style which Addison developed in these and other journals his contemporaries noted something new. Thomas Tickell, his literary protégé and first editor, thought that Addison had brought from Latin poetry into English prose a "propriety of thought and chastity of style."[10] Later in the century Joseph Warton extolled "that sweetness and purity of style"[11] which sets Addison off from earlier English prose writers. Addison wrote a conversational and informal, but carefully constructed prose which delighted whether read silently in the study or aloud in the coffeeshop.

In his lifetime the clearest sign of Addison's preeminence in literary circles was the establishment of his own Kit-Kat-like club at Button's Coffeehouse. Here the apprentice of 1704 became a master. Addison presided over the "Little Senate," not only offering to young writers poetic advice and a chance to publish but also cultivating those sentiments favorable to the Whig party. Alexander Pope was Addison's most important protégé for two years till disputes over pastoral poetry, translating Homer, and—inevitably—politics drove them apart. Pope left an indelible, but not necessarily fair, portrayal of Addison as literary patron in the "Atticus" character of 1715:

> But were there One whom better Stars conspire
> To bless, whom Titan touch'd with purer Fire,
> Who born with Talents, bred in Arts to please,
> Was form'd to write, converse, and live, with ease:
> Should such a man, too fond to rule alone,
> Bear, like the Turk, no Brother near the Throne;
> View him with scornful, yet with jealous eyes,
> And hate, for Arts that caus'd himself to rise;
> Damn with faint praise, assent with civil Leer,
> And without sneering, teach the rest to sneer;
> Or pleas'd to wound, and yet afraid to strike,
> Just hint a Fault, and hesitate Dislike;
> Alike reserv'd to blame or to commend,
> A tim'rous Foe and a suspitious Friend:

Larger than Addison's character to most contemporaries, however, were the social and political principles he espoused.

Through all his career, he never altered the themes of his work. Whether in poetry or prose, on the stage or in a half-sheet, he preached a constitutional monarchy, the Protestant succession, a secular morality founded on discipline, and a learnedness based on the best of the old and the new ideas. He sought the middlebrow, between the high and the low. Politically, religiously, socially and intellectually, Addison constructed a golden mean for his contemporaries. His citizenship balanced extremes of absolutism and republicanism, fanaticism and atheism, license and asceticism, pedantry, and ignorance. As an appropriate vehicle for his themes, Addison cultivated the middle style. Samuel Johnson succinctly defined Addison's prose: "Whoever wishes to attain an English style, familiar but not coarse, and elegant but not ostentatious, must give his days and nights to the volumes of Addison."[12]

Chapter Two

Early Criticism and Latin Poetry

The youthful writings of some authors are a clear prediction of their later and greater works; the early work of others seems unrelated to their subsequent achievement. Addison is among the first group. His early works indicate interests in and judgments of literature which will change and mature later in his career. He was convinced, like most Western men of letters before him, that literature's main purpose is to teach. He paid attention to those aspects of literature considered the most effective elements of teaching: how style and description make ideas and precepts delightful to learn.

Addison's first works reflect his major academic interest, the literature of Rome's Augustan age. Written between 1693 and 1704, they fall into two groups, critical evaluations of Latin and English poets and specimens of Latin poetry. The critical pieces are "Dissertatio de Insignoribus Romanorum Poetis" [Dissertation on the Worthier Roman Poets], "An Essay Upon Vergil's *Georgics*," "A Discourse of Ancient and Modern Learning," "An Account of the Greatest English Poets," and *Notes on . . . Ovid's "Metamorphoses."* Two Latin poems appeared in 1689; eight others were included in a collected edition, *Musarum Anglicanarum Analecta* (1699). What Addison judged to be the purposes and techniques most important to and most beautiful in the Roman poets became the material and the model for his own Latin verse.

Ornament and Style

Addison's "Dissertation on the Worthier Roman Poets" (1692), his earliest surviving essay in criticism, has all the marks of a twenty-year-old's judgment. The essay begins by remarking that Roman poets are celebrated as the world's greatest and by ranking them in poetic merit. Addison's rankings are the commonplaces of Renaissance opinion: Vergil is the greatest of all poets, the best stylist and most descriptive poet; Lucretius is the second ranking stylist, and Claudian the next best in description. Writing for an academic audience already sharing these judgments, Addison does not even bother to define such terms as style or description. By style he seems to mean diction, syntax, and tone; by description he intends the ability to create images or pictures in a reader's mind. For instance, Addison praises Vergil's *Georgics* for both qualities: *"Mira quadam Dulcedine animum ingrediatur, & quod describat, melius quam si Oculis subjiciatur, tanquam praesens intueamur."* (472) ("he captivates the soul with his wonderful sweetness, and his descriptions are as lively as if we had the object placed before our eyes.")[1] Addison's opinions presuppose another commonplace classical assumption about poetry: the most valuable is public poetry, which, like the Georgic or the epic, is concerned with moral and heroic topics; the least valuable is lyric, which expresses individual emotion.

"An Essay upon Vergil's *Georgics*" elaborates the judgments put forward in the "Dissertation." The essay is short and proceeds through four topics united around the notion, traditional in the seventeenth century, that poetry's purpose is didactic: it teaches agricultural, politicial, moral, or philosophical precepts. The first topic is the nature of the Georgic: "A Georgic, *therefore is some part of the science of husbandry put into a pleasing dress, and set off with all the Beauties and Embellishments of Poetry*" (4). The second topic is three ways the poet may embellish agricultural precepts: by suggesting ideas to the imagination instead of stating them directly, by introducing digressions for variety, and by elevating the style above common or familiar expressions. The third topic contrasts the Georgic poetry of Hesiod and Vergil and declares the latter's superiority for the "style's grandeur and gracefulness." The final topic is an evaluation of each part of the Georgics which praises especially the fourth book for its mock heroic account of the beehive in human terms.

Once again the crucial criteria to Addison are style and description. He ranks the *Georgics* as Vergil's greatest poem because of its imaginative power: ". . . we receive more strong and lively *Ideas* of things from his words, than we could have done from the objects themselves" (8). And this imaginative power allows the poem to accomplish its didactic purpose: "It raises in our minds a pleasing variety of scenes and landscapes, whilst it teaches us . . . the dryest of its precepts . . ." (4). Such is Vergil's skill that art truimphs over nature.

Approaching the same consideration from a different perspective is Addison's "A Discourse of Ancient and Modern Learning." Although not published until 1738, the context and assertions of this treatise argue that it probably dates from the 1690s. Like the *Georgics* essay, "A Discourse of Ancient and Modern Learning" does not presume much knowledge of the classics on the reader's part; it too reads like a critical primer. Its title suggests that it belongs with the essay of William Temple or the book of William Wotton as a salvo in the battle of Ancients versus Moderns. Actually, Addison does not aim to quarrel. He intends to "consider what Pleasure the Cotemporaries and Countrymen of our old Writers found in their Works, which we at present are not capable of; and whether at the same Time the Moderns mayn't have some Advantages peculiar to themselves, and discover several Graces that arise merely from the Antiquity of the Author" (449).

The advantages which the Ancients had in reading their own poetry are four. First, "they knew all the secret History of a Composure;" that is, they understood allusions to contemporary persons and events. Second, "Their being conversant with the Place, where the Poem was transacted, gave 'em a greater Relish than we can have at present of several Parts of it; as it affected their Imaginations more strongly, and diffus'd through the whole Narration a greater Air of Truth." Third, the Ancient poets wrote about the heroes of their own nations, "For by this Means they have humor'd and delighted the Vanity of a *Grecian* or *Roman* Reader; they have powerfully engaged him on the Heroes's Side, and made him, as it were, a Party in every Action." The final advantage is the Ancients' knowledge of the sound and harmony of their own language which no Modern can pretend to know accurately. Addison states that were a Modern to read ancient Greek or Latin to an Athenian or Roman, the latter would be at a loss to recognize his native tongue.

But if modern understanding is less because of ignorance of what was familiar knowledge to ancient readers, the Modern's ignorance also gives several graces to ancient poetry. First, a modern reader cannot judge failures of style because he cannot know what words were common, mean, or vulgar. All sound equally sonorous to the modern ear. The same quality is true of persons and place names: we hear only dignified syllables whereas an ancient audience would know the reality behind the sound: "How oddly therefore must the Name of a Paultry Village sound to those who were well acquainted with the Meanness of the Place." Third, a modern reader would not catch awkward or foreign constructions in the language; we "take it for granted, that the Stile is beautiful and elegant, where they find it hard and unnatural."

The modern reader obviously comes off second best to the ancient reader as an appreciator of Greek and Roman poetry despite these three advantages. The former's pleasures are found in his ignorance of the relation of sound and meaning; the latter's pleasures are based on firsthand knowledge of the objects, people, and events described by the poems. Only the modern reader who is knowledgeable in classical culture or who can rely upon a scholarly translator is going to appreciate anything of ancient poetry. The standard of literary enjoyment raised by Addison in "A Discourse" has, however, implications for his own poetic practice. If literary enjoyment depends on readers' comparing what they know with written descriptions of these things, then the subject matter for the modern writer, even of Latin verse, is obvious. (Twenty years later, the principle of familiarity underlay Addison's *Spectator* papers.) In this early essay, as in Addison's other pronouncements upon literature, the key to the art is the reader's response to the way that description and style depict familiar objects and ideas.

Although cast as a poem, "An Account of the Greatest English Poets" should be studied with Addison's early critical essays. Neither as verse nor as criticism is it very good or very persuasive. Compared with Addison's later literary criticism, the poem expresses superficial opinions: it gives little credit to Chaucer and Spencer, totally ignores Shakespeare and Donne, and praises Roscommon and Halifax, whom posterity has condemned to obscurity. But it must be remembered that the poem is, in some ways, an intentionally slight performance. Directed to a friend, "H.S." (whom some biographers identify as Henry Sacheverel), at Oxford, the poem provides with Horatian ease and good fellowship a hopefully witty and compressed summary of contemporary taste in poetry. Addison is not so much expressing his own critical preferences as repeating the attitudes common to the wits of his generation; in this respect it is much like the dissertation on the Roman poets discussed above. But whether Addison's observations carry much weight today is irrelevant; more importantly the poem reflects his concerns about literature. Like his previous works, "An Account" focuses on the language poets use and the reader's response to that language.

Addison's judgments on individual poets have a common theme; certain writers are in or out of fashion because modern readers speak or think differently from them. Chaucer, for example, is a victim of changes in the English language:

> But age has rusted what the Poet writ,
> Worn out his language, and obscur'd his wit. (11. 13–14)

Spenser falls victim to contemporary scientific mentality:

> But now the mystick tale, that pleas'd of yore,
> Can charm an understanding age no more. (11. 23–24)

Conversely, other lesser poets receive praise on grounds that have nothing to do with literary skill: Cowley is "blest" because he combines poetic competence with interest in the scientific investigations of the Royal Society; Dorset earns praise because he celebrates in his verse the military victories of King William.

These poets give readers written accounts of familiar people, events or objects.

Addison's interest in style and description carries over into his translations of Ovid. His notes to selections from the *Metamorphoses* eschew the critical tradition of arguing the rightness of mythological allusions or pointing out obscure morals. Addison prefers to point out the stylistic excellences of different passages "because I believe such a comment would give the reader a truer taste of poetry than a comment on any other Poet wou'd do" (134).

None of Addison's early critical works contains enduring judgments or observations. Addison's reputation as a critic rests on the *Spectator* papers done a decade or more later. But these five critical pieces, done in the same years as the bulk of Addison's poetry, reveal the artistic and aesthetic concerns that he found at the heart of poetry. However much we find his judgments superficial or commonplace, they do reveal Addison's interest in the imaginative impact that poetry has upon the reader. The ability to appreciate those elements of poetry which make it vivid and impressive, in turn, lays a foundation for taste, the ability to distinguish good poetry from bad. In Addison's later critical writings "taste" will hallmark the growth of the knowledgeable reader and critic.

The Latin Poetry

Soon after Addison's accession to the Demy at Magdalen his first publications, two Latin poems, appeared in print. "Tityrus et Mopse" appeared in an anthology published (1689) in praise of the accession of King William and Queen Mary. The second poem, "Gratulatio," was published in the following year in another anthology by members of the college to congratulate the king on a successful campaign in Ireland against supporters of James II.

Addison's contribution to the first volume is a dialogue between two Vergilian shepherds, Tityrus and Mopsus, who applaud the return of peace and prosperity to the country in clichéd compliments to the new king and queen. The second poem briefly recounts, in Vergilian hexameter, William's campaign in Ireland, and concludes with an exhortation to defeated James to spare the country further conflict. Both are the mediocre performances of a young man, analogous to the early critical works. Though Addison must have recognized their shortcomings and later kept them out of his collected works, they did publicly declare his allegiance to the new king.

Much more substantial and polished Latin poetry appeared in 1699 when Addison edited a volume of works from Oxford, *Musarum Anglicanarum Analecta*. Eight of Addison's own poems are included: "Ad Burnettum" [To Dr. Burnett], "Ad D.D. Hannes" [To Dr. Hannes], "Resurrectio" [The Resurrection], "Barometri Descriptio" [Description of a Barometer], "Sphaeristrum" [The Bowling Green], "Machinae Gesticulantes" [The Puppet Show], "Praelum Inter Pygmaeos et Gures Commisum" [The War Between the Pygmies and the Cranes], and "Pax Gulielmi" [William's Peace]. Although the exact date of composition for each is unknown, most were first composed in the mid-1690s and revised extensively a couple of years before publication in 1699. They are finely crafted pieces and indeed were thought by Addison's contemporaries worthy enough to earn him an international reputation as a Latin poet. As the survey of Addison's critical interest in poetry suggests, they are essentially elegant poems, ornamenting thought and displaying a virtuosity in style over seriousness of subject matter. Addison expresses the same concern in the preface to the volume, declaring that elegance of style was the major criterion for the poems he selected.

One path to elegance is imitation. "To Dr. Hannes" and "To Dr. Burnett" are both odes in the Horatian style, poems of personal compliment and written in four-line stanzas (alcaic form). The first poem is addressed to Edward Hannes, a physician and Latin poet who was Addison's contemporary at Oxford. Addison compliments Hannes by that sincerest form of flattery—imitation; he models the beginning of the poem on one Hannes had written to the pioneering physician Thomas Sydenham. Addison praises his subject for the gracefulness of his poetry and for

his skill in medicine. From imitation Addison moves to a typically
Horatian invitation:

> Et quem dierum lene fluentium
> Delectat ordo, vitaque mutuis
>   Felix amicis, gaudiisque
>   Innocuis bene temperata. (11. 41–44)
> (Pleased with a few selected friends,
>   He views each smiling evening close,
> While each succeeding morn ascends
>   Charged with delights, unmarked with woes:
> In pleasures innocently gay,
>   Wears the remains of life away.)[2]

Addison's critical theory carries over into his own practice. In his
Latin poetry one finds the ornamentation of thought by the garb
of poetry. It is an early demonstration of what Addison will
always do well—embellish ordinary thoughts so gracefully that
one almost forgets how familiar the sentiments are.

The second ode praises Thomas Burnett's controversial volume,
The Sacred Theory of the Earth. Burnett's book challenged the
traditional theories of the creation, history, and future of the
earth. By praising such a book Addison was again aligning himself
with the new thinking of the day. The poem retells in vivid
details Burnett's description of earth's fate at the final judgment:

> Exudat ardens terra fluentia
> Rivis metalla, & diluvio globus
>   Flammarum inundat, dum tremendo
>   Fluctuat omne solum tumulto. (11. 41–44)
> (Their naked tops the hills admire,
>   No longer white with fleecy dew;
> And as they moan the spreading fire
>   Add to the flames' dissolving too:
> While rocks from melting mountains flow,
>   And roll in streams through the vales below.)[3]

These descriptions alternate with hyperbolic praise for Burnett,
a characteristic that has caused L. C. Bradner to find this ode

unfaithful to its Horatian tradition: "The magnitude of the subject and the enthusiasm of Addison's praise would perhaps have found better expression in the heroic eloquence of hexameters or elegiacs than in the traditional, moderated urbanity of the alcaic ode."[4] Although unfaithful to convention, the mixture of description and compliment always appealed to Addison and marks his English poetry as well.

The delight in description that Addison valued so highly and which drives him beyond the Horatian in "Ode to Dr. Burnett" is the predominant element in four other Latin poems: "The Resurrection," "The Description of a Barometer," "The Bowling Green," and "The Puppet Show." All the poems share these two qualities. They attempt to describe familiar objects—objects likely to be among the more interesting a village curate sees—in unfamiliar terms. They gain part of their effect by the reader's ability to contrast the thing itself with its written account. This was the central advantage, according to Addison's "Discourse," for ancient readers of the Roman poets over modern readers.

Indeed the first translator of the "Resurrection," Nicholas Amhurst, gives support to Addison's theory with his account of the excellence of Addison's original Latin lines:

Nor does their only excellence consist in being an accurate poem; but also in being an exact copy of the painter's original upon the altar in Magdalen College; but so much improved with all the strongest figures, and most lively embellishments of a poetical description, that the reader receives a double satisfaction in seeing the two sister arts so useful to each other.[5]

"The Resurrection" begins with a description of the painter's formidable task in depicting the Last Judgment. It moves to a description of the painting itself, looking first at the outside edges filled with millions of damned and saved souls and then narrowing down to the center of the picture in which stands the Savior summoning all souls to judgment. The poem narrows even further to the wounds in the side of the Savior, the wounds that are the source of divine salvation. The poem concludes with a description of the terrors of the damned so lifelike that it fulfills Addison's ideal of the description which surpasses reality:

> Ut toti metuas tabulae, ne flamma per omne
> Livida serpat opus, tenuesque absumpta recedat
> Pictura in cineres, propriis peritura favillis. (11. 94–96)
> (So strong, so fierce, the painted flames arise,
> The pale spectator views them with surprise;
> Believes the blazing wall indeed to burn,
> And fears the frame should into ashes turn.)[6]

"The Description of the Barometer" is a modernized Georgic, teaching about an instrument of the sciences rather than a precept of farming. The poem tells first of how the mercury is mined, then how a barometer is made, and finally how it is read to predict the weather. The technical information is embellished by a variety of techniques: the mercury is complimented by an allusion to Jove, and weather forecasting is elaborated by descriptions of bright, fair days and dark, rainy ones. The poem concludes with a reminder, cast in homey images, of the trustworthiness of the instrument.

> Quin varios coeli vultus et tempora prodit.
> Ante refert, quando tenui velamine tutus
> Incedes, quando sperabis frigidus ignem. (11. 56–58)
> (By this the face of heaven is justly shown,
> The changes told, and all the seasons known:
> This tells you when to trust a loose attire,
> And warns you when to hope a winter fire.)[7]

Besides amplified description Addison renders the familiar in an unfamiliar fashion by the manipulation of style. In "The Puppet Show" and "The Bowling Green," sophisticated diction describes the commonplace. "The Puppet Show" describes puppets at a county fair acting out the mighty deeds of biblical characters or famous warriors. "The Bowling Green" tells of a party of bowlers who divide into teams for a friendly game. Little happens besides the expected; some bowlers strike, others miss. The fun is in the minute account of events infused with drama, passion, and personification by a deliberately distanced style. Thus Addison describes a badly bowled ball:

> Nec risus tacuere, globus cum volvitur actus
> Infami jactu, aut nimium vestigia plumbum
> Allicit, et sphaeram a recto trahit insita virtus.
> Tum qui projectit, strepitus effundit inanes,
> Et, variam in speciem distorto corpore, falsos
> Increpat errores, et dat convitia ligno.
> Sphaera sed, irarum temnens ludibria, coeptum
> Pergit iter, nullisque movetur surda querelis. (11. 36–43)
> (What sudden laughter echoes o'er the green,
> When some unlucky, artless cast is seen!
> When the too ponderous lead with stubborn force
> Allures the globe from its appointed course!
> The bowler chafes, and fruitless rage ensues,
> His body to a thousand postures screws:
> He blames he knows not what, with angry blood,
> He frets, he stamps, and damns the erroneous wood:
> The erroneous wood his fruitless rage disdains,
> And still its former wayward course maintains.)[8]

The result of such tension between subject and style is probably not more than "a mildly humorous glow,"[9] pleasant on first reading but not immortal poetry. Addison's next Latin poem, "The Battle between the Pygmies and the Cranes" is, however, probably the best of his Latin poems. The style is mock heroic, one of the most popular forms of poetry in the late seventeenth and early eighteenth centuries. Dryden, Swift, Pope, and dozens of lesser poets tried their hands at the mock heroic and gave us many great prose works and poems—e.g., "MacFlecknoe," *The Battle of the Books, The Rape of the Lock.* The form of mock heroic supposedly had classical precedent in Homer's lost "Battle of the Frogs and Mice."

Addison's poem begins with the standard invocation to the muse and an account of all the heroic deeds of six-foot men recorded in song; it then introduces its unusual topic—the heroic deeds of foot-and-a-half-high men. The action of the poem is set in India, where for years Pygmy warriors have preyed upon the eggs and very flesh of the Cranes. "Roused to vengeance by repeated wrong," the Cranes gather into a huge skyborne army for an all-out attack. The Pygmies have the better of the battle until their chief—a giant of twenty inches!—is carried off by a huge fowl. A second attack breaks the ranks of the Pygmies, who are slaughtered as they attempt to flee the field. But the Pygmies' fate is not totally tragic. Legend holds that these warriors' souls either ascended to the Elysian fields or remained on earth to become what superstitious people call fairies.

The success of "The Battle between the Pygmies and the Cranes" hinges on three factors. First, Addison manages in 159 lines most of the conventions of heroic poetry—the invocation of the muse, the epic simile, the focus on the champion warrior, the tracing of the causes of the war. Brevity here is partly the soul of the poem's wit. Characteristically, perhaps, Addison in later years counseled Pope against expanding his mock-heroic poem *The Rape of the Lock.*

The second is Addison's power of description. The descriptions range from the pathetic to the comic, but Addison's best lines play with the dichotomy between the Pygmies' size and their pretentions to greatness. The poet obviously delights in his account of the Lilliputian overconfidence of the Pygmy champion:

> Jamque acies inter medias sese arduus infert
> Pygmeadum ductor, qui majestate verendus
> Incessuque gravis reliquos sepereminet omnes
> Mole gigantea, mediamque assurgit in ulnam.
> Torvior aspectu (hostilis nam insculpserat unguis
> Ore cicatrices) vultuque ostentat honesta
> Rostrorum signa, et crudos in pectore morsus. (11. 75–81)
> (And now the monarch of the Pygmy throng,
> Advancing, stalks with ample strides along;
> Slowly he moves, majestically tall,
> Towers o'er his subjects, and o'erlooks them all;—
> A giant Pygmy, whose high spirits swell,
> Elated with the space of half an ell;
> Stern was his visage,—for his face all o'er
> Of savage claws the dire impressions bore.)[10]

The third element, Addison's humor, is evident in the previous quotation but is especially strong in the conclusion. After 150 lines of mingled desolation and comedy, how can Addison resolve the poem? How to insure that the sympathy for the dead warriors will not finally obscure the mock-heroic touches? Addison's solution is to award the Pygmies an imaginative eternity neither despairing nor glorious:

> Elysii valles nunc agmine lustrat inani,
> Et veterum Heroum miscetur grandibus umbris
> Plebs parva: aut, si quid fidei mereatur anilis
> Fabula, Pastores per noctis opaca pusillas
> Saepe vident umbras, Pygmaeos corpore cassos.
> Dum secura Gruum, et veteres oblita labores
> Laetitiae penitus vacat, indulgetque choreis,
> Angustosque terit calles, viridesque per orbes
> Turba levis salit, et lemurum cognomine gaudet. (11. 151–58)
> (Now, mixed with shades of mighty heroes slain,
> The empty troops o'erspread th' Elysian plain.
> And if th' important story be allowed,
> Confirmed by fame, each night the Fairy-crowd,
> Unbodied forms, by wondering shepherds seen,
> Skim through the gloom, and gambol o'er the green.
> With schemes of war no more their bosoms glow,
> Forget their labours, and their feathered foe;
> But sportive now in wanton dances round,
> With narrow tracks they mark the flowery ground:
> A greener turf the verdant ring supplies,
> And in the Fairy name the Pygmy dies.)[11]

Thus, Addison's "Battle," like Pope's *The Rape of the Lock,* ends happily by ending fantastically.

"William's Peace" is unlike any of Addison's other Latin poems in subject and tone, although it is like them in purpose. The subject is the end of William's war against Louis XIV by the Treaty of Ryswick; the tone is an alternating rhythm of pride in victory and rejoicing in the arrival of peace. The purpose of the poem is the glorification of England and of her warrior king. The use of Latin, of classical allusions and conventions, and of echoes from heroic poetry suggests that the poem attempts to preserve the memory of victory in an enduring form.

The poem begins by inviting King William to enjoy the fruits of peace now that warfare has ended. The poet vividly recalls the scenes of fighting: the ruined landscape across which armies surged, the heroism of English troops storming ramparts, the devastating mine explosions beneath the ramparts which blew up defender and attacker alike. Though thousands fought, the glory of the war resides primarily with William, who led the Allies and serves as a model of heroism to other monarchs such as Peter the Great of Russia, whose visit to England (1697–98) symbolizes Europe's respect for the English king. William's victory brings him home to a happy and proud people. The poem describes the reuniting of English fighting men with their wives and children, William's return to his son, whose child's-play with little forts and mock swords foretells how he will follow his father's pattern, and London's celebration of the victory with a great display of fireworks. The poem concludes with an invocation to the muses for help in preserving the fame of William and of England.

Addison ornaments the patriotic themes of "William's Peace" with classical imagery and allusion. The explosion of the ramparts is like Jove casting his thunderbolt. King William's meeting with the visiting czar is analogous to the Italian king Evander receiving the wandering Aeneas. The returning soldiers and sailors are modern Argonauts bearing the fleece and recalling their adventures in a foreign land. King William is another Achilles, wrathful against his enemies and glorying in battle. An occasional passage recalls some other Latin poem by Addison. The desolate battlefield is like the barren Pygmy kingdom, and the delightful antithesis of style—common to "The Bowling Green" or "The Puppet Show"—between elevated diction and familiar activity characterizes the description of London's public drunkenness and the fireworks spectacular which hail the king's return to England.

Two elements of "William's Peace" look ahead to Addison's English verse rather than back to his Latin poetry. The first is the trick of complimenting, as he does in the case of Peter's visit to William, by finding the apt classical parallel for a contemporary

event. The second is the image of a happy people united under
a victorious ruler, of a nation glorying in its growing power. In
future poems the image will unfailingly appear. Here it appears
as a triumphant coda to London's celebration:

> Laetitiam ingentem atque effuse haec gaudia civis
> Jam tandem securus agit, positoque timore
> Exercet ventos, classemque per ultima mundi
> Impune educit, pelagoque licentius errat:
> Seu constricta gelu, mediisque horrentia Cancri
> Mensibus arva videt; seu turgida malit olenti
> Tendere vela noto, qua thurea flamina miscet
> Aeolus, et placidis perfundit odoribus auras. (11. 167–74)
> (Each subject now, while William fills the throne,
> Springs with new life, and calls that life his own:
> To nature's bounds their fleets control the main,
> No dangers dread, and every foe disdain.
> Secure they wander; and while he is kind
> The sea no terror has, no rage the wind:
> Whether to freezing climes their course they hold;
> O'er icy waves, and bound with summer's cold;
> Or cross those oceans where perfuming gales,
> And blasts of incense, swell the driving sails.)[12]

Chapter Three
English Poetry

Addison's reading and practice of Latin poetry shaped his English verse. It inspired him to translate selections from Vergil, Horace, and Ovid and to attempt English imitations of classical models.

Addison published translations throughout his career. He began in 1694 with Vergil's fourth *Georgic* and a tale from Ovid's *Metamorphoses,* and concluded in 1717 with further translations of Ovid. The years between witnessed translations not only of Vergil and Ovid but of Horace (Book III Ode III in 1707) and of many other poets whose passages adorn the pages of *The Remarks Upon Several Parts of Italy* (1705), the *Spectator* papers (1711–1712), and *Dialogues Upon the Usefulness of Ancient Medals* (written 1701–1703; published 1721). All his translations follow a similar pattern. To provide English readers with a clear text of Latin verse which is often condensed or elliptical in expression and thought, Addison's translations add to the original idea explanatory comments and expanded images, and substitute familiar allusions for obscure ones.[1] His method, almost formulaic, yields workmanlike verse translations rather than inspired poetic adaptations. Addison translated in the same way many of his contemporaries did.

Addison did have pretensions as an English poet. His original poetry attempts to cast contemporary persons and subjects in classical patterns (especially the epistolary and heroic) of thought and expression. He wishes to be a modern Vergil, the poet who sings the nation's greatness and the greatness of men who lead her in peace and war. Often Addison captures by image, allusion, and convention the outward appearances of his model, but too often he lacks its informing spirit. Though claiming to speak for a nation, his verse usually trumpets a partisan political philosophy. The result was stagnation: his poetic method changed as little between "A Poem to His Majesty" (1695) and "To Sir Godfrey Kneller" (1716) as his commitment to the Whig party. After brief experiments with poems on literary topics, Addison always cut his verse from the same cloth.

False and Fair Starts

Addison's first published English poems are "A Song for St. Cecilia's Day 1692" and "To Mr. Dryden" (1693). The first is a young poet's piece, heavily derivative, and an experiment in a genre for which the author had no talent. The second is a better performance, in a mode akin to the Horatian ode and on a subject familiar to the writer.

"A Song for St. Cecilia's Day" was written for performance on November 22, the feast day of the legendary Cecilia, patroness of music. It was one of several presentations—homiletic, choral, and orchestral—in honor of the saint. The theme of the feast was what has been called "musical humanism," the attempt to unite the powers of music and poetry and thereby move an audience to heightened moral and religious awareness.[2] The marriage of melody and words symbolized an ideal relationship between man's two natures: the intellect harmonized with the emotions, reason harmonized with passion. Dryden's St. Cecilia's Day ode for 1687 had immediately become the standard for all subsequent celebrations of the saint. Addison modeled his song on Dryden's, just as he patterned his Latin verse on classical models. Imitation may be the sincerest form of flattery, but it invites invidious comparison upon the copier. Although one of Addison's contemporaries professed that "the words of this piece are extremely fine, well adapted to the day, and exactly fitted to the Musick,"[3] modern taste finds the "song" a hodge-podge of poetical clichés and Dryden echoes.[4]

Like Dryden, Addison writes four irregular stanzas and a chorus. The first stanza invokes St. Cecilia's inspiration for the singers and musicians; the second catalogues their instruments of praise. The third stanza retells Orpheus' power of music; the fourth proclaims music's grace to raise the soul to God. All these parts down to the Orpheus allusion are found in Dryden's poem. Addison's limitations as a lyric poet are well illustrated in his "Song." He sinks just when he ought to rise. Two examples should make the point. First, in the climactic stanza the Deity whom man is aspiring to reach by song is described as "well pleased and courted with a song" as if He were a wealthy but bored patron in need of entertainment. Second, when, in that same stanza, Addison describes the end of the world, he prosaically mentions what Dryden etches in condensed language and striking image. Dryden writes:

> So when the last and dreadful hour
> This crumbling pageant shall devour,
> The trumpet shall be heard on high,
> The dead shall live, the living die,
> And Musick shall untune the sky.
> ("A Song for St. Cecilia's Day 1687" 11. 59–63)

Addison echoes:

> When Time itself shall be no more,
> And all things in confusion hurl'd,
> Music shall then exert its pow'r
> And sound survive the ruines of the world. (11. 49–52)

The more successful "To Mr. Dryden" reveals a poet in control of his material. Abandoning the lyric mode for which he had not the spirit, Addison turns to the poetic epistle which echoes the tone and attitude of his Latin Horatian odes. The model is more the ode to Dr. Burnett than the one to Dr. Hannes; compliment and flattery are more obvious than the call to good fellowship and *memento mori*. The reason undoubtedly hinges on the subject of the poem, John Dryden. Dryden is an established, famous poet and Addison is an unrecognized university scholar; according to the social etiquette of the day, Addison could not address Dryden casually. Addison compliments by two devices, the use of classical parallels and hyperbolic praise. His handling of poetic style shows his attention to the polite or correct couplet which stresses the continuity of thought rather than antithesis.[5]

In "To Mr. Dryden" Addison turns Dryden's unfortunate social and political state from an occasion of lamentation into an occasion of praise. In 1693 Dryden was an aging poet, once laureate to Stuart kings but now an outcast after the 1688 Revolution. Addison finds a classical parallel in the circumstances of Ovid, the first century Roman poet in exile because of Augustus Caesar's displeasure with some explicit love poetry. Addison's compliment is doubly sly. Like Ovid, Dryden had written many erotic songs which lost favor when the court of William III disavowed the licentiousness of Charles II's court; Dryden was also engaged upon a translation of Ovid's *Metamorphoses*. According to Addison, Dryden has managed to triumph in circumstances that overwhelmed Ovid. The British laureate's "second youth is kindled" with fresh poetic productions where the Roman, "pensive and sad," lost all inspiration.

Addison's second technique of compliment is hyperbolic praise. Dryden has so well translated all of the great Roman poets— Juvenal, Vergil, Persius, and Horace—that

> Thy Copy casts a fairer Light on all,
> And still out-shines the bright Original. (11. 19–20)

The poem concludes on a similar note; Dryden's latest translations of Ovid will dazzle even the original poet:

> Then will thy *Ovid,* thus transform'd, reveal
> A Nobler Change than he himself can tell. (11. 35–36)

In the eighteenth-century view, all artists perfect Nature. According to Addison, Dryden, the consummate artist, perfects the perfectors.

As a handler of the dominant poetic meter of the age, the iambic pentameter couplet, Addison reveals himself in this poem no mean practitioner but certainly not the equal of Dryden, Pope, or Johnson. His purpose is not to startle the reader with a striking revolution of thought but rather to lead the reader logically from one line to the next. The second lines of the couplets just quoted, for instance, grammatically as well as logically complete the first lines. In the polite couplet the first line often contains the subject and the verb, while the second line provides the object. Alternatively, the second line may be a restatement of the thought of the first line. Addison's correct couplets usually work together in pairs or triplets like the paragraphs of a simple but cohesive freshman composition: the first stating a thesis, the next supporting the thesis by elaboration or examples. In short, the technique, style, and organization of "To Mr. Dryden" mark it the prototype of Addison's major original poems in English. It is not a poetic style which modern taste readily appreciates, but one which contemporaries thought gave to English poetry an ease and clarity which it had long lacked.

"And Poetry in Higher Thoughts Is Lost"

Addison's five major English poems span twenty years (1695–1716), yet show a uniformity of subject and style. Like "To Mr. Dryden" each poem addresses an eminent person at some crucial military or political moment. "To the King" (1695) celebrates William III's victory at Namur. "A Letter from Italy" (1701) consoles Charles Montagu, Addison's patron, who lost his post in William's government. "The Campaign" (1704) eulogizes John Churchill for leading the Allied army to victory over France at the battle of Blenheim. "To Sir Godfrey Kneller" and "To Her Royal Highness" (1716) praise the succession of the house of Hanover to the English throne.

To the personal compliment which characterizes "To Mr. Dryden" these poems add the expression of nationalistic, Protestant feeling. They celebrate through classical images and conventions (especially from Vergil and Claudian) the struggle of Protestant heirs to the throne to surmount the commercial and military might of France abroad and the sentiment for Stuart monarchy at home. Addison expressed this combination of the personal and the public in the preface of "To the King." In times of national crisis, "Poetry in higher thoughts is lost." It presumes to speak with one public voice about the ambition and destiny of a whole people.

The national statement of "To the King" is the celebration as fact what was in 1695 only a hope that England was a nation united under its king. The country was as divided by party disputes as it had been in the 1680s. William's war against Louis XIV was not going well; the victory at Namur in 1695 which occasioned Addison's poem was William's first victory since the Boyne in 1689. At sea, the navy had won a victory at LaHogue, but the merchant fleet was suffering heavy losses to French privateers. The expense of the war and the degree of English commitment on the Continent were unsettling, as were the unresolved questions about the Anglican Church and the competition of landed and commercial interests. The nation was divided by many issues which Addison chose to ignore in his description of William's landing in England at the conclusion of that summer's campaign:

Well-pleas'd, thy People's Loyalty approve,
Accept their Duty, and enjoy their Love.
. . . .
So crown'd with Laurels now, where-e're you go,
Around you blooming Joys, and peaceful Blessings flow. (11. 217–24)

To elevate this vision from partisan hope into the measured and calculated expression of a national will, Addison dresses the poem in classical garb.

Unlike other odes of the 1690s Addison's does not allow any humorous touch to break the solemnity of "To the King." It begins with a lament that William's heroic deeds, like Aeneas' or Achilles', may wait a thousand years for a Vergil or Homer to sing their glory in verse. Apparently William fights with divine sanction:

> The Race of Nassaus was by heav'n design'd
> To curb the proud Oppressors of mankind. (11. 55–56)

The king earns the traditional epithet "god-like," and the French are called by the name of their barbarian forefathers, "Gauls."

A spectacular but ineffective naval bombardment of the French coast rises above military mediocrity by an epic simile which compares the cannon fire to the eruption of Mt. Aetna (11. 155–69). To the authority of the classics and Providence is added that of English history. The troops who storm and capture Namur gain inspiration from the memory of their forefathers' victory at Agincourt (11. 65–72). The sailors who bombard the coast recall the seamen who defeated the Spanish Armada (11. 111–14).

William's heroics, the will of heaven, and martial valor combine to ensure English liberty and prosperity. The sign of victory is expanded commercial activity:

> Where-e'er the Waves in restless errors rowle,
> The Sea lies open now to either Pole:
> Now may we safely use the *Northern* gales,
> And in the *Polar Circles* spread our sails;
> Or deep in *Southern* climes, Secure from wars,
> New Lands explore, and sail by Other stars;
> Fetch Uncontroll'd each labour of the Sun,
> And make the product of the World our own. (11. 115–22)

The generalized diction and paraphrase of these lines stress the ideal of freedom rather than the reality of profits which follows improved trade.

"A Letter from Italy" arranges the same ingredients of personal compliment, classical learning, and political meditation in a slightly different form. The poem is Addison's epistle to Charles Montagu, the patron who secured the pension which allowed him to travel the Continent. Patron and poet are similarly placed at the moment, one retired from the government and one distant from England. But though leisure allows the poet to compose and the patron to read these verses, higher thoughts eventually claim attention. "A Letter from Italy" progresses from landscape to compliment to political insight.

The first forty lines report the encounter of the scholar with the land he knows so well through his beloved poets:

> Poetick fields encompass me around,
> And still I seem to tread on Classic ground. (11. 11–12)

The tour provides the aesthetic pleasure which "A Discourse of Ancient and Modern Learning" described as essential to poetry. Addison compares the physical landscape of rivers, monuments, and battlefields with the classical poets' accounts of them. The comparison confirms the principle that art perfects Nature, that poetry awards an immortality or greatness to objects not naturally magnificent. Viewing the Tiber, Addison realizes (11. 41–43) that poetry has made a simple stream greater in repute than the Danube or Ister.

The next score of lines praises Montagu for his poetic efforts to immortalize William's victory at the battle of the Boyne. The memory of William's heroic struggle reminds the poet of England's responsibility for the maintenance of European liberty. The last section of the poem contrasts Italy with England. The first is blessed with natural abundance but suffers under French occupation:

> But what avail her unexhausted stores,
> Her blooming mountains, and her sunny shores,
> With all the gifts that heav'n and earth impart,
> The smiles of nature, and the charms of art,
> While proud Oppression in her vallies reigns,
> And Tyranny usurps her happy plains? (11. 107–12)

The second, by contrast, possesses a cool climate and rocky soil, but is a happier land. Thanks to valorous kings and steady statesmen Liberty "crowns Britannia's isle / And makes her barren rocks and bleak mountains smile" (11. 189–90).

The poem concludes on a familiar note: England, united under William, must stand firm against "bold presumptuous kings" like Louis XIV. Fifteen years later "To Sir Godfrey Kneller" and "To Her Royal Highness" celebrate a different Protestant king in similar terms. Like "A Letter from Italy" both poems move from personal occasion to statements of political faith.

The full title explains the first poem: "To Sir Godfrey Kneller on His Picture of the King." Godfrey Kneller, court painter since the time of Charles II, painted a portrait of George I to celebrate his accession. Addison finds the conjunction a happy one; the perfect painter has captured the soul of the perfect monarch:

> The magick of thy art calls forth
> His secret soul and hidden worth.
> His probity and mildness shows,
> His care of friends, and scorn of foes:
> In every stroke, in every line,
> Does some exalted virtue shine,
> And *Albion*'s happiness we trace
> Through all the features of his face. (11. 7–14)

In 1716, public relations pieces like Kneller's portrait and Addison's poem were desperately needed. Many Englishmen failed to see a promising monarch in a man who did not speak his subjects' language, who brought with him courtiers and mistresses used to German rather than English manners, and who ended the long sequence of Stuart monarchs. But Addison is sure that King George indeed possesses all the virtues which Kneller's art captures on canvas. When his people see George as Kneller does, they will gladly hail the new sovereign: "And crowds grow loyal as they gaze" (1. 22).

Addison reinforces this familiar vision of the happy nation with compliments based on classical mythology. First there is a bit of ancient alchemy: "The genial sun" has refined gold so that it may be privileged to be stamped with George's profile on coins and medals. Second, Addison finds an analogy to the present in the history of the past. The last quarter of the poem compares Kneller to the Greek sculptor Phidias, who undertook to carve all the gods from Pan to Jove. In a brilliant paralleling of myth and English history, Phidias' lecherous Pan, gloomy Saturn, warlike Mars, childless Minerva, mournful Thetis and powerful Jove become Kneller's portraits of the libertine Charles, the deserter James, the warrior William, the lovely Mary, the troubled Anne, and the challenged George. What higher classical compliment could Addison offer than to identify George I with Jove, who ended rebellion among the gods? Those eager to hear the dignity and inevitability of the Protestant succession stated must have thought what Richard Hurd later put into words: "There never was anything happier than this whole illustration, nor more exquisitely expressed."[6] Like Jove, George in 1716 beat down the rebels.

"To Her Royal Highness" is a necessary companion of "To Sir Godfrey Kneller." The latter celebrates the present of the Protestant succession; the former poem celebrates its future. Her Royal Highness is Caroline, daughter-in-law of George I, wife of the prince who will become George II, and mother of the children who will follow their father to the throne. The poem is full of compliment traditional to women: praise of her beauty; praise of her virtues which will become models for heroines of the stage; and flattery of Caroline's children, of daughters who will break young princes' hearts and of a son who is destined to rule with charm and wisdom.

In the final compliment rests the meaning of the poem. Addison takes here the same stand that he took in "Tityrus et Mopse" (1689). England's destiny lies with a strong Protestant succession; when the poet sings of daughters and sons, he sings as well of "the prospect of successive reigns" without the threat of a Stuart return. In "To Her Royal Highness" the person addressed is less the real subject than the hope that a new royal family ends a "broken lineage, and a doubtful throne."

Such hyperbolic praise as these four poems bestow upon kings, queens, and counselors probably did more to confirm Addison's place as the Whigs' best panegyric poet than they did to sway popular sympathy. No doubt Addison's poems filled the vital need of giving an image of order and of rightness in moments of national crisis. What is damaging to Addison's reputation as a poet is that too many of the conventions, the phrases, and the images are alike. Between 1695 and 1716 he was content with competency.

"The Campaign"

"The Campaign" (1704) illustrates the dictum that it was the Whigs' prerogative to praise war and the Tories' to praise peace.[7] Like "To the King," "William's Peace," and "A Letter from

Italy," it commemorates a stage of England's fight against Louis XIV. For once Addison had a subject worthy of classical and heroic ornamentation. Marlborough's campaign in Germany and the victories at Schellenberg and Blenheim were an epic event. Marlborough marched his large army across territory on a scale that awed his allies and his enemies alike. In these battles more than 100,000 men were engaged, half of whom became casualties. The battles shattered the myth of French military invulnerability. In the cliched but occasionally accurate phrase, Blenheim was a decisive battle of history.[8] So Addison wrote the poem with which the ministry of Sidney Godolphin welcomed home the conquering hero John Churchill, Duke of Marlborough.

"The Campaign" is a narrative poem. It begins, after an invocation to the muse, with an account of Louis XIV's threat against Germany, whose King Leopold appeals to England for aid. These appeals launch the Duke of Marlborough and his armies on a campaign deep into Germany. After a long march, the British army defeats the French first at Schellenberg and then at Blenheim. The poem recounts the military consequences of the victory and summarizes the final stages of the campaign. It concludes with an apostrophe to England's greatness and a hope that the poem will prove worthy of its subject.

Two themes dominate "The Campaign." Like his other political poems, it treats the events of 1704 as an occasion to celebrate the dignity and majesty of the British nation. England under Queen Anne is like England under William III, the protector of Europe from the tyranny of Louis XIV:

> To *Britain*'s Queen the Nations turn their eyes,
> On her resolves the western world relies,
> Confiding still, amidst its dire alarms,
> In ANNA's councils, and in CHURCHILL's arms.
> Thrice happy *Britain,* from the kindoms rent,
> To sit the guardian of the continent! (11. 29–34)

Addison's second theme is more important. The poem asserts that the nation's greatness rests upon the greatness of one man, the Duke of Marlborough, John Churchill. When Addison writes in the invocation that he is "transported with a theme so new," he emphasizes that he celebrates a new type of hero, the man of common rank become ennobled. John Churchill, the son of a politician knighted for his loyalty to Charles II, had begun his acquaintance with aristocracy as a page and with the military as an ensign. His personal bravery in battle and his ability to lead troops advanced him to higher ranks, first in the military and consequently in the aristocracy. The hero of epic verse is traditionally a prince or a king, noble by the very fact of birth; Addison intends to sing of the man who rises to a position of power on the "firm basis of desert."

The centrality of this new theme is signaled in the first epigraph from the Latin poet Claudian's panegyric "On Stilicho's Consulship" (Book III): "In his case all discord among the different classes has ceased; the Knight rejoices, the Senator applauds, the people's prayers rival the support of the Patricians." Stilicho, although not a native Roman aristocrat, virtually led the western empire in the late fourth century. By negotiation and warfare he kept at bay the barbarians who threatened Rome. In Asia, Africa, and Europe Stilicho was constantly on campaign for two decades against threat after threat. At times his success was threatened by discord and intrigue at court by those envious of an "upstart's" achievement. "The Campaign" suggests to the English that Marlborough, their Stilicho, deserves praise from both Whigs and Tories for success in the land warfare against Louis XIV.

Throughout the poem Marlborough is pictured as worthy of heroic stature traditionally accorded the warrior of noble blood. It is his "mighty scheme" to lure the French armies into battle; it is his love of liberty and courage in battle that inspires the troops. In battle he stands out amid the heaving and dying masses of soldiers, like the portrait of a man seen against a backdrop of numerous small figures. At Blenheim,

> 'Twas then great MARLBRO's mighty soul was prov'd,
> That, in the shock of charging hosts unmov'd,
> Amidst confusion, horror, and despair,
> Examin'd all the dreadful scenes of war;
> In peaceful thought the field of death survey'd,

> To fainting squadrons sent the timely aid,
> Inspir'd, repuls'd, battalions to engage,
> And taught the doubtful battel where to rage. (11. 279–86)

Marlborough's military genius earns him equality with royalty. When he meets the Austrian commander Prince Eugene for the first time (11. 101–14), the two men strike an instant friendship. After the victories at Schellenberg and Blenheim, the English general becomes the tutor as well as friend of the prince:

> The royal youth by MARLBRO's presence charm'd,
> Taught by his counsels, by his actions warm'd,
> On *Landau* with redoubled fury falls,
> Discharges all his thunder on its walls,
> O'er mines and caves of death provokes the fight,
> And learns to conquer in the Hero's sight (11. 425–30)

Marlborough's ascension to traditional heroic status is complete when "Increas'd with titles, and with conquests crown'd," he receives from the Hapsburg empire the gift of a principality and the title of prince.

"The Campaign" is obvious in its political statement, praise of England's leadership on the Continent, and panegyric to the man who embodies that leadership. But what about "The Campaign" as poetry? Once highly praised, the poem is now regarded as unreadable. The basic criticism is immortally etched in Joseph Warton's label, "that gazette in rhyme."[9] So faithful is the poem to the sequence of marches and battles that Addison seems not to have shaped his material with any artistry beyond the usual classical trappings of an opening invocation and a heroic epithet. Critics have always claimed that Addison's couplets march as dully as Marlborough's troops: one foot routinely follows another. The poet fails to capture the passion or horror of war; there is pose rather than action.[10] Addison's verse hovers uneasily between poetry and prose; the poet applies "ornaments" from the outside to straightforward, expository statements—rather like a painter applying gilt trim to a sturdy white cottage.

Limited as the poetic achievement may be, "The Campaign" is not a mean performance. It is important to realize that Addison, writing in the months directly after the battles, faced difficult problems. He had to deal with recent events, well known to readers from newspaper and pamphlet accounts. Unlike heroic poets who write of mighty deeds long ago, Addison is confined to actions not yet remote enough to acquire a ready dignity just by being ancient. He is stuck with a sequence of historical events which he must remain faithful to and render with dignity. Many poets tried in 1704 and 1705 to solve the same problems and won immediate obscurity. Addison did better.

One way to approach the poem is to suggest why "The Campaign" is better than the poems by Daniel Defoe, John Dennis, Matthew Prior, and others. There are two reasons for "The Campaign's" preeminence: its length and its organization. For one thing it is less than five hundred lines long, enough to tell the story and apportion praise. Most competitors were significantly shorter or longer. The shorter ones remain so general in their praise that they could be about almost any event; they have little more to do than look about them and die. The longer ones must necessarily develop elaborate machinery or compliments; they stagger like troops on an endless march, until they collapse of exhaustion. A poet like John Dennis delights in sheer absurdities, as when British troops are raked by cannon fire:

> Their mangled Trunks divided from their Limbs:
> Yet all their dauntless Spirit they retain.[11]

Addison's poem is restrained in comparison with those of Blenheim laureates who heap classical trappings, in the manner of Addison's previous poems, upon the persons and events. Marlborough receives the epithet "god-like" once or twice, and Prince Eugene's claim "that in the pagan gods his lineage ends" resounds only once. Only once are the two generals compared to classical warriors. Similes are reserved for crucial moments in the poem and are drawn from natural rather than unfamiliar similarities. Marlborough's march into Germany in search of battle with the French army is likened to a hunt:

> So the stanch Hound the trembling Deer pursues,
> And smells his footsteps in the tainted dews,
> The tedious track unrav'ling by degrees:
> But when the scent comes warm in ev'ry breeze,
> Fir'd at the near approach, he shoots away
> On his full stretch, and bears upon his prey. (11.121–26)

The ferocity of battles at Schellenberg (11. 129–51) is described in terms of an elemental struggle in Nature. To describe the retreat of the defeated French army Addison returns to the image of the hunt, but now from the perspective of the prey:

> But soon as the victorious host he spies,
> From hill to hill, from stream to stream he flies:
> Such dire impressions in his heart remain
> Of MARLBRO's sword, and *Hocstet*'s fatal plain:
> . . . .
> They fly the conqueror's aproaching fame,
> That bears the force of armies in his name. (11. 399–406)

The only extravagant image finds the analogy to Marlborough's personal direction of battle in divine providence:

> So when an Angel by divine command
> With rising tempests shakes a guilty land,
> Such as of late o'er pale *Britannia* past,
> Calm and serene he drives the furious blast;
> And, pleas'd th' Almighty's orders to perform,
> Rides in the whirl-wind, and directs the storm. (11. 287–92)

If the simile verges on blasphemy, it is at least quickly done.

To keep to the known facts of the campaign and at the same time to aim higher than a newspaper account, Addison gives the poem a clearly defined structure. This poetic organization aims to reflect the purposefulness of Whig policy and of Marlborough's strategy. Addison overcomes the handicap of being tied to a sequence of events—and to a sequence of dull marching at that—by balance. Balance here means elements of consistency and variety, of comparison and contrast, of narration and analysis. The poem is meticulously organized into parallel sections. The opening (11. 1–12) and concluding (11. 463–76) sections express the poet's conventional hope that his poem will do justice to this subject. The second (11. 14–46) and penultimate sections (11. 443–62) contrast the oppressive and tyrannical French with the liberty-loving English. The poem divides into halves at lines 207–18, on the fulcrum of an invocation to Louis XIV to give up his mad dreams of conquest after Marlborough's first victory. Each half of the poem treats a major battle: Schellenberg (11. 127–96) and Blenheim (11. 249–360). As noted above, one distinctive natural simile decorates each battle. Each battle is preceded and followed by an account of the British line of march, controlled by the image of the hunt. Each half of the poem recounts a visit by Eugene of Savoy to Marlborough's camp (11. 99–114, 407–24). The balancing and paralleling keep in simultaneous view the particular events of 1704 and the larger issues of the European war.

Addison remains faithful, however, to more than just the sequence of marches and battles. He remains just as faithful to the actions and personality of the hero, both when they conform to epic pattern and when they do not. Marlborough's complaints about the heat and dust, which gave him headaches on the march, receive a mention—albeit poeticized into "chaf 'd Temples"— in "The Campaign." The image of the Angel to describe Marlborough's control of the fighting, while stylized, agrees in substance with what eyewitnesses and historians say about his personal direction of troops. Likewise, Marlborough's lament (11. 225–38) at loosing a scorched-earth policy upon Bavaria, whose elector refused to surrender after Blenheim, echoes what the duke wrote to his wife, Sarah, at the very moment he inaugurated the policy of burning and tearing down: "This is so uneasy to my nature that nothing but an absolute necessity could have obliged mee to consent to itt, for these poor pepel suffers onely for their master's ambition [sic]."[12]

Addison's "Campaign" is not the demythologized war poetry that modern readers have come to expect. But it is by no means a dishonest account of the events of that summer of 1704. If the poem cannot be read with the enthusiasm its contemporaries gave, it can still be accepted as a dignified and stylized expression of national pride. If it is not a poem that rises to immortality, it is "a highly appropriate summary of the march and battle and a fine tribute to a great field general."[13]

Chapter Four
Early Prose Works

Addison's first significant prose works, after the few critical essays that came out of his university studies, show the same dual interests as his original English poems. Addison directs his knowledge of classical culture and his classically formed style to the presentation of Whig political ideas. The mixture is essentially the same whether the political theme grows gradually out of some other subject matter or whether the piece is designed for a specific political occasion. *Remarks Upon Several Parts of Italy* and *Dialogues Upon the Usefulness of Ancient Medals* fall into the first group; "The Present State of the War," the *Whig-Examiner,* and "The Trial of Count Tariff " fall into the second group. Although in the early 1700s original prose works in English did not compare favorably with poetry as a means to literary immortality, Addison revealed in prose a defter touch than in verse.

Addison showed little progress as a poet. Both in Latin and English verse, he succeeded almost at once to a fair level of competency and never went beyond it. His career in prose was different. Although the content of his works never varied significantly—he remained devoted to Whig principles, genteel theology, Stoic morality, and a gentlemanly code all his life—Addison did show a growing artistry in the presentation of ideas. No two works in this early period were writen for the same occasion or audience or relied on the same techniques. Addison, by choice or by necessity, wrote in a variety of tones and devices to present his sentiments. In the process he demonstrated that his best style was casual, humorous, and replete with apt details. Later in his career, when he became involved in periodical journalism, he found himself in a medium where these qualities were demanded not on occasion but every day.

Remarks Upon Several Parts of Italy

Remarks Upon Several Parts of Italy in the Years 1701, 1702, 1703, as the title suggests, records Addison's visits to cities up and down the Italian peninsula, but also includes his observations on places in Switzerland and Austria. The book ends oddly; it just stops after an account of the city of Halle. Addison may have intended, but never wrote, a second volume on his travels in Austria and Germany. Though the *Remarks* is lightly regarded today, it was highly prized in the eighteenth century. Travel literature—which records the times, places, institutions, and people which inevitably change—is a difficult genre in which to achieve literary immortality. Those travel books which achieve distinction, like Boswell and Johnson's accounts of the Hebrides, usually do so because they reveal as much about the visitor as the visited. Addison's *Remarks* has very little about the traveler himself, but it clearly reveals his interests. Addison "has traced out for us in his observations a very perfect map of his own mind."[1] That mind in 1705 was filled with classical learning and concerned with the political situation of England. Addison's *Remarks,* unsurprisingly but uneasily, is at once a guidebook and a commentary.

Basically, Addison writes for the benefit of fellow travelers, armchair or actual. He records in the manner of a modern guidebook what sights are worth seeing in each of the cities he visits. He comments upon historical sites or landscapes, buildings, statuary, inscriptions, paintings, or collections of antiquities. Addison pays special attention to curiosities and rarities (a copy of a sermon St. Francis supposedly preached to fish) and to items that would interest Englishmen (the tomb of a medieval English knight or a letter from Henry VIII to Anne Boleyn in the Vatican library). Addison's *Remarks* is a volume a tourist could take along for guidance or dip into for amusement.

Every guide to travelers seeks to be distinctive. Addison used his knowledge of classical history and literature to ornament and distinguish his text. He explains in the Preface:

For my own part, as I have taken notice of several Places and Antiquities that nobody else has spoken of, so, I think, I have mentioned but few things in common with others, that are not either set in a new light, or accompanied with different reflections. I have taken care particularly to consider the several passages of the ancient Poets, which have any relation to the Places and Curiosities that I have met with. (18)

The practice comes naturally to Addison, who in his earliest comments on literature emphasized the pleasure which a reader draws from comparison of an object with its description. In the *Remarks* recalling appropriate classical passages takes precedence over telling of his personal adventures. When a storm drives his ship into the harbor at Monaco, Addison reports little about the tempest; instead he quotes a description of the port from a classical poet:

Lucan has given us a description of the Harbour that we found so very welcome to us, after the great danger we had escaped.

> *Quaque sub Herculeo sacratus nomine portus*
> *Urget rupe cava pelagus: non Corus in illum*
> *Jus habet aut Zephyrus: Solus sua littora turbat*
> *Circius, et tuta prohibet statione Monaeci.* Lib. I
> The winding rocks a spacious harbor frame,
> That from the great *Alcides* takes its name:
> Fenc'd to the west, and to the north it lyes;
> But when the wind in southern quarters rise,
> Ships, from their anchors torn, become their sport,
> And sudden tempests rage within the port. (21)

Addison's intention to use "several passages of the ancient Poets" was an underestimate. In the course of his *Remarks,* he quotes from nineteen poets more than two hundred selections to help him describe the landscape, cities, and artifacts of Italy. He uses his vast knowledge of classical poets as a modern reader would use a road map: "The greatest pleasure I took in my journey from *Rome* to *Naples* was in seeing the fields, towns and rivers that have been described by so many *Classic* Authors, and have been the scenes of so many great actions" (94). For good or ill, these quotations from the Latin poets quickly came to dominate readers' impressions of *Remarks Upon Several Parts of Italy.* Horace Walpole complained that "Mr. Addison traveled through the poets, and not through Italy."[2] The extensive quotations and generalized descriptions also made Addison's observations seem vague enough that Samuel Johnson observed many sections "might have been writen at home."[3] The most casual tourist could have equalled Addison's descriptions of the amphitheater at Verona: "There is something very noble in it, though the high wall and corridors that went around it are almost entirely ruined, and the Area is quite filled up to the lower seat, which was formerly deep enough to let spectators see in safety the combats of the wild beasts and gladiators" (42). Too many of his descriptions are this bland.

Delightful as Addison found the experience of comparing classic ground with ancient descriptions, he did not travel as an idle observer. The cities he toured were both the battleground between Louis XIV and England's ally the Hapsburg empire and a spectrum of political systems from republics to tyrannies. Like other men on the tour for political education, Addison measured the strengths and weaknesses of other governments against those of his own. In terms of Addison's early aesthetic, the description of antiquities and landscapes by classical quotation or by personal observation ornaments and makes pleasant the precepts about religion, government and society. Addison's *Remarks,* like his poems of this decade, concerns the Protestant cause and England's political stability.

Thus, the lesser half of the *Remarks* is a tour-guide to ancient Italy. Political commentary is the heart of the book. Though an orderly discussion of its political comments might suggest a fully developed political philosophy presented in the guise of a travel book, Addison's observations are frequent but scattered throughout. They reflect not a system of thought but a set of assumptions about the well-ordered and prosperous state. Addison's political comments are as random as those on rivers, paintings, or valleys that occur as the author travels from city to city. Only a few cities attract attention as political entities, but these few generate the most sustained discussions and unified sections of the *Remarks*.

Just as he describes curiosities especially appealing to his countrymen, Addison relates political matters of most concern to Englishmen in 1700. These topics include the superiority of Protestantism over Catholicism, the role of commerce, and the spirit of free states. Here is the prosaic version of the topics ornamented in Addison's political poems.

Like "A Letter from Italy," the *Remarks* contrasts a tyrant's land filled with Nature's bounty to a free land ill-blessed by Nature.[4] Part of the land's misery results from the deprivations of occupying French troops. Another reason for the poverty of a land possessing fertile soil and mild climate is its religion, Roman Catholicism. After recounting the geographical and climatic advantages of the Papal states, Addison analyzes the cause of the people's obvious wants:

there is not a more miserable people in *Europe* than the Pope's subjects. His state is thin of inhabitants, and a great part of his soil uncultivated. His subjects are wretchedly poor and idle, and have neither sufficient manufactures, nor traffick to employ them. These ill effects may arise, in a great measure, out of the arbitrariness of the government, but I think they are chiefly to be ascribed to the very genius of the *Roman catholick* religion. . . . (93)

To Addison Catholicism is a religion which abuses individuals by superstitious beliefs and societies by misdirected energies and resources. Gothic cathedrals are pointed examples of Catholicism's abuse of society:

When a man sees the prodigious pains and expence, that our forefathers have been at in these barbarous buildings, one cannot but fancy to himself what miracles of Architecture they would have left us, had they been only instructed in the right way; for when the devotion of those ages was much warmer than that of the present, and the riches of the people much more at the disposal of the Priests, there was so much money consumed on these *Gothic* Cathedrals, as would have finished a greater variety of noble buildings, than have been raised either before or since that time. (176)

There are, however, political and economic factors as well that determine prosperity. Not unexpectedly Addison finds that those states which have an active commercial life and a public-spirited nobility—those states most like England—possess the keys to domestic tranquility and economic health. His observations on contrasting pairs of cities confirm the Whig prescription for the unified and successful state.

Early in the *Remarks* Addison devotes a long paragraph to the Bank of Genoa. In the 1690s England had founded a similar bank which successfully financed William's long war against Louis XIV. The Bank of Genoa, too, has become its state's surest support, able to repay debts "Whatever inconveniencies the state laboured under" (25). Like the Bank of England it has been attacked by aristocratic interests, but those interests are selfish and unconcerned with the nation: "It is however very certain, that the people reap no small advantages from it, as it distributes the power among more particular members of the republick, and gives the commons a figure" (25). Prosperity and balanced political power are the fruits of the bank.

Venice's commercial situation stands in contrast to Genoa's. With easy access to the sea and fortunately placed for Mediterranean trade, Venice ought to have a flourishing economy. But commerce lags because the state taxes trade heavily and because the "Nobles think it below their quality to engage in traffick" (53). The result is a lessened commerce and concomitant inability to confront rival nations. A nation, like Venice or England, that fate has suitably placed for trade must accept its destiny or suffer the consequences. The Venetians "are tenacious of old laws and customes to their great prejudice, whereas a trading nation must be still for new changes and expedients, as different junctures and emergencies arise" (53). Venice is the decaying maritime power England would be if it did not challenge the commercial dominance of France. Venice is the Tory recipe for England.

Besides religion and commerce, public spirit affects the life of a state. For Addison the models of the proper attitude are the small republics of Lucca and San Marino. Both are remarkable, independent enclaves among the numerous Italian states subject to France or Spain. Addison's opening description of Lucca (181) stresses the devotion of the citizens to liberty, a devotion reflected in their careful cultivation of every inch of land. The account of San Marino concludes with a striking picture of the fruits that flow from a love of freedom even when prosperity must be won from a harsh landscape:

> The people are esteemed very honest and rigorous in the execution of justice, and seem to live more happy and contented among their rocks and snows, than others of the *Italians* do in the pleasantest vallies of the world. Nothing indeed can be a greater instance of the natural love that mankind has for liberty, and of their aversion to an arbitrary government, than such a savage mountain covered with people, and the *Campania* of *Rome,* which lyes in the same country, almost destitute of inhabitants. (75–76)

In contrast to these well-ordered and freedom-loving city-states is again Venice, a state ruined by dissension and private interest. Once looked to by all of Europe for centuries as the home of republican liberty and commercial daring, as a small, independent state able to resist absorption into more powerful, larger empires, and as a secular society keeping religion out of politics, Venice seemed to have lost all her virtues to factions which put private fortune above national policy. With stinging sarcasm Addison describes the ways in which the Republic is preserved:

> To encourage idleness and luxury in the Nobility, to cherish ignorance and licentiousness in the Clergy, to keep alive a continual faction in the common people, to connive at the viciousness and debauchery of convents, to breed dissentions among the Nobles of *Terra Firma,* to treat a brave man with scorn and infamy; in short, to stick at nothing for the publick interest, are represented as the refined parts of the *Venetian* wisdom. (57)

To a Whig Venetian wisdom is unfortunately Tory wisdom. No other passage in the *Remarks* is written with such sarcasm and anger because no other passage expresses such heartfelt partisanship.

Although it clearly reflects his classical and political preoccupations, the *Remarks* does not reflect Addison's literary ability.

The book simply begins and simply ends; no prologue or epilogue gives it shape or unifies the author's impressions. Nor are passages selective. Instead of ignoring uninteresting topics, Addison troubles the reader with the fact: "At *Ferrara* I met nothing extraordinary" (66). Worst of all, the prose style ranges from mediocre to poor. It is undistinguished writing from a man who soon became renowned for his fluent prose. The style is as plain as a freshman's account of "How I Spent my Summer" and equally prey to redundancies and tautologies which often plague writers who have little to say. Even worse, the style is often grammatically incorrect. A contemporary reviewer was so struck by Addison's flawed prose that he published an annotated list of errors:

p. 1	*Beautiful garden gives a pleasing Prospect.* (Agreed, at any time of the Year)
pp. 20–21	*"Same" us'd as an Adjective Relative without any Antecedent.* (Send him back to school again)
p. 150	*An Aquaeduct that conveys Water* (Not Fire)
p. 240	*Have went.* (Fetch me the Rod)[5]

The chastened author never repeated such lapses.

Dialogues Upon the Usefulness of Ancient Medals

Although not published until Tickell's edition of Addison's works (1721), *Dialogues Upon the Usefulness of Ancient Medals* also grew out of the European tour. His interest in Roman coins was stimulated by three factors: his love of things classical, the coin collections he had seen at Paris and Rome, and preparation for work at the English mint should his patron secure him a position there.[6] The book may also result from the enforced leisure of his travels. From Rome Addison wrote to Edward Wortley, "I am forc'd for want of better company to converse mostly with pictures statues and Medals: for You must know I deal very much in Ancient Coins and can count out a Sum in Sesterces with as much Ease as in pounds sterling."[7] Of all Addison's works about classical literature, the *Dialogues* is his piece of true scholarship.[8]

The *Dialogues* records the conversations of three young Oxford scholars, Cynthio, Eugenius, and Philander. The first dialogue occurs as the trio strolls along the Thames. Philander attempts to convince Cynthio and Eugenius that the study of ancient medals (commemorative as well as ordinary coins) is a legitimate intellectual pursuit. The second dialogue, the longest and the central discussion, depicts the scholars seated at tea and studying several trays of medals. Philander leads his companions from medal to medal as he observes the characteristic and importance of each. (The reader consults several pages of plates which illustrate the medals.) The third and shortest dialogue, perhaps unfinished, compares the merits of ancient and modern medals.

Like the *Remarks Upon Several Parts of Italy,* the *Dialogues* displays the wealth of Addison's classical knowledge. He uses anecdotes from Roman history and quotations from Roman poetry to explicate the figures or words impressed on a coin. On other occasions he reverses the process: the coin's illustrations help to understand historical events or explicate literary passages. Addison realized, of course, that such coin-by-coin analysis was a dry subject. Writing to George Stepney, he noted how the study of coins, "that is in itself very bare of ornaments," needed to be handled "divertingly."[9] Addison therefore chose the dialogue form, apparently modeling his work on Fontenelle's *Dialogue on the Plurality of Worlds* (1686), which discusses modern physics in a form readable by a generally educated but scientifically untrained man or woman. The dialogue form was, according to the Augustan concept of the teaching purposes of art, a device for insinuating truth into the reader's mind without a formal delivery.[10] The dialogue form gives a structure to Addison's thought, a structure that his travel book lacks.

Addison's dialogue is a drama in miniature. Each speaker has a distinctive personality: Philander is knowledgeable about coins but hesitant to appear pedantic; Eugenius is amiable and ready to learn; Cynthio is wittily skeptical about any bother over old pieces of metal. Although each dialogue eventually turns into a lecture by the expert (with Eugenius and Cynthio, like well-rehearsed actors, asking the right questions to bring out Philander's knowledge) Addison provides an occasional lively and clever exchange between advocate and antagonist. Early in the first dialogue Philander explains that the rarity of the coin, not its metallic content, determines its value; this standard invites and receives the obvious rejoinder from Cynthio:

It is the Device that has raised the species, so that at present an *As* or an *Obolus* may carry a higher price than a *Denarius* or a *Drachma*; and a piece of mony that was not worth a peny fifteen hundred years ago, may now be rated at fifty crowns, or perhaps a hundred guineas. I find, says *Cynthio,* that to have a relish for ancient coins it is necessary to have a contempt of the modern. But I am afraid you will never be able with all your Medallic eloquence, to perswade *Eugenius* and my self that it is better to have a pocket full of *Ortho's* and *Gordians* than of *Jacobus's* or *Louis d'ors.* (283–284)

In the two passages cited, Addison's style seeks to make the learning more delightful. It is easy and conversational, largely free of technical terminology.[11] Nor are Cynthio's skeptical comments frequent enough to become interruptive or to compete with the main subject for the reader's attention. Similarly Addison gives minimal attention to establishing the setting for each dialogue: there is just enough to give the reader a sense of place and mood, yet leave the mind free to concentrate on the topic. For example, Addison begins Dialogue II with a passage which delights as much for the brevity of setting as for the writer's humorous self-awareness:

Some of the finest treatises of the most polite *Latin* and *Greek* writers are in Dialogue, as many very valued pieces of *French, Italian,* and *English* appear in the same dress. I have sometimes however been very much distasted at this way of writing, by reason of the long prefaces and exordiums into which it often betrays an Author. There is so much time taken up in ceremony, that before they enter on their subject the Dialogue is half ended. To avoid the fault I have found in others, I shall not trouble my self nor my Reader with the first salutes of our three friends, nor with any part of their discourse over the Tea table. We will suppose the *China* dishes taken off, and a Drawer of Medals supplying their room. *Philander,* who is to be the Heroe of my Dialogue, takes it in his hand, and addressing himself to *Cynthio* and *Eugenius:* I will first of all, says he, show you an assembly of the most virtuous Ladies that you have ever perhaps conversed with. (299)

Addison's attention to the readers' concerns—his assumption that writer and readers have common concerns—clearly differentiates this style from that in the *Remarks*. The writer here is at ease in giving instructions and strives to please. By comparison the style of the *Remarks* is hurried and distant.

Addison also keeps interest by arranging each dialogue about an issue. The first dialogue pits silly antiquarianism against intelligent historical appreciation. Old coins are not valuable as antiques but as sources of knowledge about ancient people's appearance, dress, instruments of war, artworks, and history. The second dialogue contrasts the symbolic interpretations which medieval and early Renaissance commentators gave to the pictures and words engraved on the coins with the modern historical and literary understanding. The third dialogue balances the Romans' clear purposes for coining medals with the haphazard and puerile motives behind French and English coinage of them. Ancient coins were struck to celebrate great events in peace or war, to praise the nation and its leaders, and to instill civic pride through appropriate images and inscriptions. Modern coinage too often marks trivial events, flatters a leader through fulsome compliment, and dresses figures in pseudoclassical garb or quotes pretentious tags of poetry. In each dialogue the discussion always flows from the less intelligent to the more intelligent position and from the general and remote to the specific and immediate. If Addison's concern with the political implications of coinage seems eccentric now, it was not so in the early 1700s. In 1704 James Coningham published *A Critical Essay on Modern Medals*, which discussed coins struck in honor of the Duke of Marlborough. Coningham interpreted the device and the inscription unfavorably in regard to Marlborough, whose friends regarded the book as a libel. [12]

Finally, the arrangement of the dialogues is a hierarchical one. The third dialogue does not compare ancient and modern coinage simply to award distinction to the superior civilization. The comparison points out that modern society has not taken advantage of a way to publicly embody its values and its dignity. Care in production and design would make coinage a testimony, like buildings or literature, to civilization: "We ought to look on Medals as so many monuments consigned over to Eternity, that may possibly last when all other memorials of the same Age are worn out or lost. They are a kind of Present that those who are actually in Being make over to such as lie hid within the depths of Futurity" (389).

For Addison this concept had practical as well as theoretical application. In March 1705 he submitted to the treasury a proposal for a new coinage to be struck after the union of England and Scotland.[13] The original proposal is lost, but part of it became the basis of *Guardian* 96. Addison advised that the impressions on farthings and half-pence record the "most remarkable parts of her Majesty's reign."

By this means, medals that are, at present, only a dead treasure, or mere curiosities, will be of use in the ordinary commerce of life, and, at the same time, perpetuate the glories of her Majesty's reign, reward the labours of her greatest subjects, keep alive in the people a gratitude for public services, and excite the emulation of posterity. To these generous purposes nothing can so much contribute as medals of this kind, which are of undoubted authority, of necessary use and observation, not perishable by time, nor confined to any certain place. . . .[14]

Political Pamphleteering

The position in Godolphin's administration which "The Campaign" brought Addison also brought him the responsibility of defending the administration's policies in times of crisis. First in 1707 and again in 1710, Addison put aside other duties or literary projects to present the Whig position in print.

In November 1707 Addison wrote "The Present State of the War." It argues that despite recent reverses on the battlefield, England must continue to prosecute the war against France. Addison's pamphlet is an elaboration of the position enunciated in the House of Lords by the Whig leader Sir John Somers: "no peace can be honourable or safe for her majesty and her allies if Spain and the Spanish West Indies be suffered to continue in the power of the House of Bourbon."[15] "The Present State of the War" has two sections. The first argues the reasons why the war should continue; the second argues that England has the resources to successfully prosecute the war. Since most of the pamphlet marshals facts and figures about manpower, finances, and like considerations, there is little opportunity for Addison to ornament precepts. In a time of crisis and decision there is no leisure to search for apt allusions or employ classical conventions.

Yet there are a few rhetorical touches in "The Present State of the War," and all of them aim to reinforce the pamphlet's conclusion that England's success depends mainly on her people's willingness to bear the short-run burdens which inevitably bring forth the fruits of victory. Since the willingness to sacrifice is an emotion that can be stirred, Addison used his rhetorical skills in allusion, imagery and style to persuade his readers.

The two classical allusions in the pamphlet are both, predictably, from Roman military history rather than from Roman poetry. Each is strategically placed in the essay to sum up an argument. The first occurs midway through as Addison completes the review of why England must continue to fight France: "It was a celebrated part in *Caesar*'s character, and what comes home to our present purpose, that he thought nothing at all was done, while anything remained undone" (248). The second allusion comes near the end of the essay after Addison has analyzed England's means to conduct the war: "The old *Roman* General, when he heard his army complain of thirst, shewed them the springs and rivers that lay behind the enemy's camp" (262–63). Classical history provides precedent and proverbial wisdom that those who dare to be great must have the will to endure.

The images by which Addison illustrates most of his arguments are short, vivid, and familiar analogies. To argue that France's modest increases in wealth and power are reason to attack more aggressively instead of growing more cautious, Addison comments, "If these little by-currents, that creep into the country by stealth, have so great a force, how shall we stem the whole torrent, when it breaks in upon us with its full violence?" (243). A nautical image attempts to refute the concept that England bears too much of the war's burden and her allies too little: "Supposing a multitude embarqued in the same vessel, [in which] there are several that in the fury of a tempest will rather perish than work for their preservation; would it not be madness in the rest to stand idle, and rather chuse to sink together than do more than comes to their share?" Both of these images, as well as others in the pamphlet, are rhetorical questions. The form, as well as the image, attempts to persuade by suggesting the obviousness and inevitability of the writer's position.

The other striking feature is a style that is occasionally heightened, almost oratorical in effect. Early in "The Present State of the War," Addison recasts Somers's principle in Ciceronian rhythms and balanced phrases:

Let it not therefore enter into the heart of any one that hath the least zeal for his religion, or love of liberty, that hath any regard either to the honour or safety of his country, or a well-wish for his friends or posterity, to think of a peace with *France,* till the Spanish monarchy be entirely torn from it, and the house of *Bourbon* disabled from ever giving the law to Europe. (244–45)

Just as he expanded his translations of Latin phrases, here Addison has particularized and imaged each part of the Whig leader's statement in the House of Lords.

This ability to state his party's principles and policies in stirring language was once again employed in the late summer of 1710. The Whigs of Sidney Godolphin's administration had lost the favor of Queen Anne and were in the process of being replaced by a Tory administration. In such circumstances public relations were important for each party: for the Whigs to preserve as much power as possible and for the Tories to acquire as much as possible. A Parliamentary election scheduled for October would be crucial in determining the relative strengths of the parties. The Tories had a public voice in the journal *Examiner,* whose expressed purpose was to examine a "great variety of papers, neither so correct, so moral, nor so loyal" and thereby "set the people right in their opinions."[16] For the Whigs, Addison—newly experienced in periodical journalism by his contributions to Richard Steele's *Tatler*—embarked on the *Whig-Examiner* to do the same thing.

Between September 7 and October 12, Addison wrote five issues of the *Whig-Examiner*; when the elections ended, the journal ceased publication. Each of the five issues took up a current topic of the political fighting. *Whig-Examiner* 1 attempts to rebut *Examiner* 6, which had attacked Samuel Garth's poem in praise of Godolphin and had offered in its stead a riddle disparaging the cast-out Whig minister. *Whig-Examiner*s 2 and 4 make fun of a brief publication entitled "A Letter to the *Examiner*," which had praised the Tory journal for attacking the "Factious Cabal" of Whig leaders who had prolonged the war.[17] *Whig-Examiner* 3 demonstrates how Addison put his knowledge of ancient politics to work for a contemporary politician; he retells the election speech of Alcibiades, a Greek general, as representative of the views of James Stanhope, a Whig candidate for Parliament. *Whig-Examiner* 5 is a political manifesto reiterating, at election time, the principles on which the Whigs justified their support of the constitutional monarchy of the Protestant succession and their opposition to the absolutism of the Stuarts. The party could use a writer skilled in a variety of styles.

But he offered another ability as well, his talent for humor. It shows well in *Whig-Examiner*s 2 and 4, which ridiculed the logic and language of "A Letter to the *Examiner*." In the former paper Addison argues that the "Letter" is hardly an objective, nonpartisan confirmation or endorsement of the methods and ideas of the Tory paper:

This crying up of the Examiner's antidote puts me in mind of the first appearance that a celebrated quack made in the streets of Paris. A little boy walked before him, publishing with a shrill voice, *Mon pere guerit toutes sortes des maladies,* "My father cures all sorts of distempers"; to which the doctor, who walked behind him, added, in a grave and composed manner, *L'enfant dit vrai,* "The Child says true."[18]

In the latter issue Addison diminishes his opponent by classifying it in a pseudogenre of literature, the genre of nonsense. The classification becomes delightful as Addison launches into a mock scholarly discussion of the genre's types (high and low).

Low nonsense is the talent of a cold, phlegmatic temper, that in a poor, dispirited styl creeps along servilely through darkness and confusion. A writer of this complexion gropes his way softly amongst self-contradictions, and grovels in absurdities. Videri vult pauper, et est pauper. He hath neither wit nor sense, and pretends to none. On the contrary, your high nonsense blusters and makes a noise, it stalks upon hard words, and rattles through polysyllables. It is loud and sonorous, smooth and periodical. It has something in it like manliness and force, and makes one think of the name of Sir Hercules Nonsense in the play called the Nest of Fools. In a word, your high nonsense has a majestic appearance, and wears a most tremendous garb, like Aesop's ass clothed in a lion's skin.[19]

Addison concludes this scholarly distinction with an amusing metaphor:

Low nonsense is like that [small beer] in the barrel, which is altogether flat, tasteless, and insipid. High nonsense is like that in the bottle, which has in reality no more strength and spirit than the other, but frets, and flies, and bounces, and by the help of little wind that got into it, imitates the passions of a much nobler liquor.[20]

Passages like these won Addison a reputation in a new genre: "Soon after their [the *Examiner*'s] appearance, came out a Paper from the other side, called the *Whig Examiner,* writ with so much Fire, and in so excellent a Stile, as put the Tories in no small pain for their favourite Hero. . . ."[21]

The witty political argument in prose proved a more congenial field for Addison than the expression of a national voice, garbed with classical conventions and echoes, in poetry. His next political pamphlet, "The Late Tryal and Conviction of Count Tariff " (1713), is a delightful triumphing over the Tories and the *Examiner.* Like his previous works, it was occasioned by a specific event, a vote in Parliament on the French and the Spanish Commercial Treaties. These treaties were proposed by Tories as part of a plan to end the War of the Spanish Succession. The treaties sought to make France and Spain England's major trading partners in place of Portugal, which had been England's ally during the administration of Godolphin. In a showdown vote on June 18, Parliament rejected the treaties, and Addison wrote to commemorate the first Whig legislative victory since 1710.

Addison casts the Parliamentary debate in the parable of a trial. Goodman Fact, representing the Whig view, has brought a suit for slander against Count Tariff, who stands for the Tory position. The Count's slanderous remarks are the arguments which the Tories used in support of the treaties and the rebuttals they offered to the Whig arguments against the treaties. Or in the language of the parable, the Count is charged with "caluminies, aspersions, and misrepresentation." The success of the pamphlet lies in the vividness and minuteness with which it depicts the issues of the treaty debates in the characters and language of a trial.

Goodman Fact is the embodiment of everything which Whigs think their party stands for and which makes England great. Every detail in Goodman Fact's manners, dress, and speech suggests both the self-confidence with which the Whigs hold their opinions and the stands which they take on the issues of encouraging domestic industry, developing foreign trade, and keeping faith with allies abroad and in the City of London:

Yet so great is his natural eloquence, that he cuts down the finest orator, and destroys the best-contrived argument, as soon as ever he gets himself to be heard. He never applies to the passions or prejudices of his audience: when they listen with attention and honest minds, he never fails of carrying his point. He appeared in a suit of *English* broadcloth, very plain, but rich. Everything he wore was substantial, honest, home spun ware. His cane indeed came from the *East-Indies,* and two or three little superfluities from *Turkey,* and other parts. It is said that he encouraged himself with a bottle of neat *Port,* before he appeared at the tryal. He was huzzaed into the Court by several thousands of *Weavers, Clothiers, Fullers, Dyers, Packers, Calenders, Setters, Silkmen.* . . . (267–68)

The portrait of Tariff suggests all that is opposite. The Count's speech is full of fancy phrases but lacks substance. His brocade coat, "curiously embroidered with Flower-de-luces," gives away his sympathy with the French and his distance from the concerns of Englishmen. Support for him comes from a defense witness dressed in a Spanish habit which seems rich but is found "nothing but show and beggary" and which characterizes how much profit England might expect from the Spanish in any commercial treaty.

But the portrayal of the Count's final defense witness, the Examiner, is the high point of the pamphlet. His introduction into the trial is a little out of place because another journal had argued the Tory position on the Commercial Treaties.[22] This passage is primarily an attack on Jonathan Swift who had written the *Examiner* for eight months after the 1710 election. Swift's *Examiner*s had to justify the new Tory ministry and denigrated the previous government. Addison's description presents the Whig viewpoint that the Examiner had enjoyed the political triumph too much and flung aspersions too freely at the fallen ministers—and even at their defenders, the Whig writers, whom he had called "perpetual Snarlers." Addison gets revenge by reducing the Examiner to nothing but a hurler of invective, as

a person who had abused almost every man in *England,* that deserved well of his country. He called Goodman *Fact* a lyar, a seditious person, a traytor, and a rebel; and so much incensed the honest man, that he would certainly have knocked him down if he could have come at him. It was allowed by everybody, that so foul-mouthed a witness never appeared in any cause. Seeing several persons of great eminence, who had maintained the cause of Goodman *Fact,* he called them ideots, blockheads, villains, knaves, infidels, atheists, apostates, fiends, and devils: never did man show so much eloquence in ribaldry. (271–72)

Examiner's speech insults the court and he must slink away before he finds himself on trial for slander.

The rhetorical strategy of the passage is superb; it outdoes in gusto and telling detail the rest of the parable. The temptation to triumph over one who had effectively lampooned the Whig ministry was irresistible. The telling placement of the phrase "that deserved well of his country" is ironically Swiftian. The very length of the string of vituperative names which the Ex-

aminer tosses about becomes comic rather than convincing, self-
revealing rather than crushing. Here, as in all good satire, the
victim hangs himself.

Chapter Five
The *Tatler*

If Addison had written only the poems and prose works discussed in previous chapters, he would be remembered today only as one of many political writers in Queen Anne's reign. Thanks to Richard Steele's enterprising journalism, however, Addison discovered a literary medium for which he had a genius rather than a competency. Steele's *Tatler* offered sophisticated Londoners reports on the latest news in politics, fashion, theater, and romance; the reports were regular, lively, and restricted to a couple of thousand words. Addison's skills, as his early writings show, shone in short rather than long works. His delight in verbal portraits of things familiar to the reader, his care to adorn instruction in delightful dress, and his range of learning and interests are the talents required in a periodical which had to first acquire and then retain a wide readership from issue to issue. The proportional shares of Steele and Addison in the *Tatler* are not precisely clear even today. Undoubtedly it was Steele's journal, but ultimately—as Steele himself said with justifiable pride—"whatever Steele owes to Mr. Addison, the public owes Addison to Steele."[1] Only after he served as Steele's apprentice did he become his own master.

Addison and Steele are commonly called periodical essayists. The latter term can be misleading. Although some *Tatler*s are like the essays of Francis Bacon or Michel de Montaigne, most of them are not what modern readers understand as essays: expository, nonfictional accounts of an idea or personal experience. *Tatler*s are in fact no one kind of writing. Some are mere summaries, and some are essays; but others use a wide range of fictional devices from the ancient fable to what we now call the short story. The *Tatler* papers were successful in the eighteenth century and remain impressive today for the variety of topics, tones, and techniques that Addison and Steele were able to arrange in constantly fresh combinations. By adding the deep resources of art to journalism, they pioneered literate entertainment.

A Different Journal

Hundreds of news-sheets, journals, and periodical papers catered to Augustan London's desire to read about the latest happenings in politics or literature, the latest ideas in religion or learning. On April 12, 1709, a new one appeared. It was called the *Tatler,* a happy choice which succinctly suggested racy and gossipy content. The first four issues were given away free in order to establish a readership. The following issues cost one penny. For his money the reader received a single folio sheet, printed on both sides, its columns filled with foreign news, political reports, stories of the goings-on between belles and beaux, and like material. The *Tatler* appeared three times a week: Tuesday, Thursday, and Saturday.

Though the writer of the *Tatler* called himself Isaac Bickerstaff, the paper's author was Richard Steele. An energetic and enthusiastic man, Steele had just been passed over for a political appointment after several years of service to the Whig administration of Godolphin. He launched the *Tatler* in hopes of achieving the two goals nearest his heart: to make money and to influence public behavior. The first goal needs no explanation, but the second deserves some comment. Steele's experience in shaping his fellow man included two years (1707–1709) as editor of the *Gazette,* the official organ through which the Junto Whigs explained and defended the policy of their administration. Like the *Gazette*—which Steele continued to edit alongside the newer journal—the *Tatler* aimed to promulgate what Steele considered moderate political principles and to provide the latest domestic and foreign news. But the new periodical also had the broader purpose of reforming the morals and manners of London and paying attention to developments in literature, especially the theater. The reformation of manners had been Steele's concern since the publication of his *The Christian Hero* (1705) which sought to provide an ethical antidote to the libertine morality that was the heritage of the Stuart reign. Steele's new type of comedy, exemplified by *The Funeral* (1701), sought to salvage, with sentiment and morality, the English stage, which had been savagely and successfully attacked as a cesspool of lewdness and profanity by critics like the preacher Jeremy Collier.

To distinguish the new journal from the many then available, Steele hit on two techniques. The first was to create a fictional editor-author, and name him Isaac Bickerstaff.[2] Bickerstaff had been originally created by Jonathan Swift in 1708, in a series of pamphlets designed to ridicule the astrologer and almanac-maker John Partridge. The first Bickerstaff pamphlet astrologically predicted Partridge's death; the second pamphlet purported to record his predicted demise. When Partridge published his next almanac and boasted that he was alive, a third pamphlet appeared to ironically and comically controvert the claim. The exchange between Bickerstaff and Partridge kept London laughing for months. In the clever, irrefutable, and popular Bickerstaff, Steele had an appropriate voice to speak authoritatively on a wide variety of subjects. Bickerstaff did not plan to mince words; he intended his papers

principally for the use of political persons, who are so public-spirited, as to neglect their own affairs to look into transactions of state. Now these gentlemen, for the most part, being persons of strong zeal and weak intellects, it is both a charitable and necessary work to offer something whereby such worthy and well-affected members of the commonwealth may be instructed, after reading, what to think.[3]

Steele began with the mocking spirit characteristic of Swift's Bickerstaff; the *Tatler* itself may at first have been intended as a mock newspaper.[4]

Steele's second distinguishing technique provided a method of presenting his various topics. He created departments to handle different kinds of subjects.[5] He geared these departments to the London clubs, theatrical world, and political centers that he knew so well; not only were they Steele's world but they were the world of his readers: Coffee-houses, taverns, and chocolate-shops were the places where Englishmen of Queen Anne's reign concluded business deals, had clothes fitted, and argued which poems and plays were best.[6] Bickerstaff explains the system of division:

All accounts of gallantry, pleasure, and entertainment shall be under the article of White's chocolate-house; poetry, under that of Will's coffee-house; learning, under the title of the Grecian; foreign and domestic news, you will have from St. James' coffee-house; and what else I have to offer on any other subject shall be dated from my own apartment. (*Tatler* 1)

All these places were the favorite haunts of Richard Steele, man about town.

This division had great advantages at first. If two or three different accounts filled an issue, no one item need be very long— a concern when one man was producing three issues a week of the *Tatler* and editing the *Gazette* as well. Friends could submit a section or a poem which Steele could insert directly under a heading or around which he could build a frame. The system of divided entries lasted for about a hundred issues before giving way to entire issues from one department. Partly the reason for the change was practical: the news features, which had at first helped sell the *Tatler*, Steele diverted exclusively to the *Gazette*.[7] Partly the reason was literary: Steele was increasingly assisted by Addison.

The *Tatler* quickly became the most popular periodical in London. Its readership increased enough by the end of 1709 that a second printing of each issue was required. The *Tatler* in 1710 had a circulation of over 3,000, a figure unheard of for a London paper. Another sign of success was the amount of advertising space which was sold; some issues in late 1710 had between fourteen and eighteen advertisers.[8] Perhaps the surest sign of success was the multiplicity of imitators. By July the exploitatively titled *Female Tatler* appeared, and in the next two years, *Titt for Tatt*, the *Tatling Harlot*, and the *Whisperer*, among others, were unsuccessful, shortlived attempts to capitalize on Steele's formula.[9]

Despite the steadily increasing success of the *Tatler*, Steele unexpectedly ceased publishing it. On January 2, 1711, he amazed his readership with an address under his own name and an announcement that he had grown tired of telling readers "what to think" on this, that, and the other topic:

But to inquire into men's faults and weaknesses has something in it so unwelcome, that I have often seen people in pain to act before me, whose modesty only makes them think themselves liable to censure. This, and a thousand other nameless things, have made it an irksome task to me to personate Mr. Bickerstaff any longer; and I believe it does not often happen that the reader is delighted where the author is displeased. (*Tatler* 271)

Most readers did not believe Steele's explanation. John Gay says that they preferred to think that he had run out of material, or that he "lay'd it down as a sort of Submission" to the Tory government which had recently come to power and which had been attacked in *Tatlers* 236 and 239, or that he intended to start a new journal.[10] Perhaps all three considerations mattered more or less.

But whatever his reasons, Steele gracefully acknowledged the help of another in many of the *Tatlers*:

The hand that assisted me in those noble discourses upon the immortality of the soul, the glorious prospects of another life, and the most sublime ideas of religion and virture, is a person who is too fondly my friend ever to own them; but I should little deserve to be his, if I usurped the glory of them. I must acknowledge at the same time that I think the finest strokes of wit and humour in all Mr. Bickerstaff's lucubrations, are those for which he is also beholden to him. (*Tatler* 271)

The friend who combined talents in "noble discourse" and "wit and humour" was Joseph Addison.

Junior Partner

Addison's share in the *Tatler* amounts to only one-fifth. He wrote forty-nine issues completely by himself and contributed a share in twenty-two other numbers. Addison's whole contributions to the *Tatler* are concentrated in two periods: thirty numbers in the winter of 1709–10 and seventeen in the late summer of 1710. These issues appeared while Addison was in London rather than in Ireland. His duties as secretary to Lord Wharton kept him in Dublin from April through July while the Irish Parliament met. Addison's partial contributions occur mainly at the beginning and the end of the *Tatler*'s run.

As few as the jointly authored papers are, they do show a change. At first, shared issues seem almost accidental: the founding editor giving his friend a chance to show his wit, the friend helping out the busy editor who needed constantly new material for his columns. The department structure facilitated slipping in a small piece by Addison. In *Tatler* 42, for instance, Steele publishes under the heading of St. James' Coffee-House Addison's humorous inventory of the props from Drury Lane Theatre (e.g., "a new moon, something decayed") in addition to entries from "My own Apartment" and "Will's Coffee-House." Joint issues done late in the *Tatler*'s run are true cooperative efforts. *Tatler*s 253, 256, 259, and 265, "the Proceedings of the Court of Honour," give no structural indication of different authors. If a reader wants to guess which writer contributed which idea or phrase, he must rely on his impressions of Steele's tone or Addison's style.

Cooperation between Steele and Addison in publication was not a new development in 1709. When Steele became editor of the *Gazette* in 1707, he worked under Lord Sunderland's office, where Addison was chief secretary. Steele secured the foreign news for the *Gazette* to publish from Addison, who received and read the diplomatic dispatches from Europe.[11] In the *Tatler*, however, aside from the joint issues, their literary cooperation was irregular and informal. There is no evidence that they planned specific matters for development in their separate *Tatler*s.[12] They were more likely to pick up and develop each other's ideas and themes when their imaginations ran dry or when a device proved popular. For instance, Steele uses material in *Tatler*s 20 and 93 from letters which Addison had written while on his European tour.[13] Addison's *Tatler* 24 continues a discussion of social types begun in Steele's *Tatler* 21. Steele develops in *Tatler*s 178 and 232 the character of the Political Upholsterer, which Addison began in *Tatler*s 155 and 160. In *Tatler* 214 Steele uses the satiric device of the Political Barometer, which Addison varies in *Tatler* 220 to the Church Barometer to comment on religious behavior.

Within the cooperation, however, Addison and Steele maintained respective spheres. Steele had a defined circle of interests—the theater, domestic manners, and politics—corresponding to his other publications—plays, moral treatises, and pamphlets. Addison had other concerns: the classics, natural religion, the concept of enlightened citizen. Never at odds, Steele and Addison's divergent interests contributed to making the *Tatler* a source of pleasure to its readers, who looked forward expectantly and unknowingly to whatever the next issue would bring. Addison's first full contribution shows how he could work within Steele's schema, pick up characteristic methods and themes, and yet add his distinctive interests and style.

Tatler 24 clearly links up with previous issues. "From White's Coffee-House" continues an analysis of social types which began in *Tatler* 21. There Steele had described the Gentleman and promised descriptions of several other types; Addison provided two of them, the Very Pretty Fellow and the Toast. "From St. James' Coffee-house" gave more foreign news. "From my own Apartment" contained a poem submitted by a reader, a poem satirizing Louis XIV's delay in signing the Treaty of Paris; this poem complemented a similar one by Bickerstaff himself in the previous *Tatler*.

Despite the similarities, especially in the last two sections, *Tatler* 24 displays a characteristic Addisonian touch in its handling of the social type. Steele's Gentleman, in *Tatler* 21 is in the tradition of the "Character." The gentleman, given the Latinate name Sophronius, is sketched with a series of general statements: he has good judgment, cheerful spirit, and superior understanding. Although Addison indicates that he will continue the characters mentioned in *Tatler* 21, his portraits of the Very Pretty Fellow and the Toast are handled differently.

Addison's sketches are more developed than Steele's. Instead of discussing one general example, Addison offers three classes of Very Pretty Fellows and eight instances. The classes are given distinguishing characteristics and the specific examples are given names which range from the realistic Colonel Burnet to the allegorical Hogshead, Culverin, and Musquit to the stereotypical Tom Drybones. This complexity of examples allows for the use of entertaining and illustrative details. For instance, commenting on the drinking habits of Very Pretty Fellows, Addison tells of three brothers recently arrived from Holland and practicing cultivated behavior for their entrance into the world:

This fraternity is preparing for our end of the town by their ability in the exercises of Bacchus, and measure their time and merit by liquid weight, and power of drinking. Hogshead is a Prettier Fellow than Culverin by two quarts, and Culverin than Musquet by a full pint. It is to be feared, Hogshead is so often too full, and Culverin overloaded, that Musquit will be the only lasting Very Pretty Fellow of the three. (*Tatler* 24)

In another instance, Addison quickly traces the career of Very Pretty Fellows in "very daring adventures in love" from virility to impotence to venereal disease with a series of representative names: "Jo Carry, for his excessive strength and vigour; Tom Drybones, for his generous loss of youth and health; and Cancrum, for his meritorious rottenness."

In his portrait of the Toast, the lady whose beauty is drunk by a gaggle of wits assembled for supper, Addison extends the character by first giving a pseudolearned account of the custom's origin and then moralizing upon the meaning of the ceremony and offering contrasting portraits of two Toasts, Mrs. Gatty and Mrs. Frontlet. Mrs. Gatty is a passionate and eager mistress while Mrs. Frontlet is aloof and difficult to stir. The addition of the moralizing commentary to the lighthearted account of manners is typically Addisonian in its use of vivid detail to ornament a familiar moral theme, the transitoriness of glory:

When she [a Toast] is regularly chosen, her name is written with a diamond on a drinking-glass. The hieroglyphic of the diamond is to show her, that her value is imaginery; that of the glass to acquaint her, that her condition is frail, and depends on the hand that holds her. This wise design admonishes her, neither to overrate nor depreciate her charms; as well considering and applying, that it is perfectly according to the humor and taste of the company, whether the toast is eaten, or left as an offal. (*Tatler* 24)

Tatler 24 typifies those of Addison's essays most like the pattern which Steele set for his journal. It mixes a detailed and acute observation of a social phenomenon with a commentary drawing a light but definite moral. So does *Tatler* 116, the trial and condemnation of a new fashion in petticoats. *Tatler* 121 is a rebuke to ladies who bestow more affection on their lapdogs than on human beings. *Tatler* 192 presents the petty disagreements of passengers in a coach on a long journey as an image of married life. *Tatler* 248 tells how Bickerstaff 's possession of Gyges' ring, rendering him invisible, allows him a nocturnal tour of London bedrooms, where he sees the secret dissatisfactions of rakes and coquettes. Manners and morals in tandem mark each of these quintessential *Tatler* essays. The moral positions are usually conventional, but what enlivens the pieces are the novel, unconventional perspectives from which the morality is proclaimed.

Tatler 100 is an excellent example. Its theme is that justice cannot always be expected in life, that the rich will not always deserve their wealth, that heroes will be neglected while cowards are favored. The moral observation comes in a dream in which Bickerstaff observes the goddess of Justice come to set the world right. She possesses a mirror which obliges anyone who sees his reflection to acknowledge his true state. One of her redistributions forces children to seek out their real fathers:

This put a great part of the assembly in motion; for as the mirror moved over them, it inspired every one with such a natural instinct, as directed them to see their real parents. It was a very melancholy spectacle to see the fathers of very large families become vacant, and bachelors undone by a charge of sons and daughters. You might see a presumptive heir of a great estate ask blessing of his coachman, and a celebrated toast paying her duty to a valet de chambre. Many under vows of celibacy appeared surrounded with a numerous issue. This change of parentage would have caused great lamentation, but that the calamity was pretty common; and that generally those who lost children, had the satisfaction of seeing them put into the hands of their dearest friends. (*Tatler* 100)

It is a commentary on the sexual mores of society done with a narrative and dramatic vividness, with gentle comedy and sharp irony.

Addison's procedure is in accord with the notion of Bickerstaff as the "Censor of Great Britain." Bickerstaff's office, as proclaimed in *Tatler*s 144 and 162, is modeled on the Roman Cato, who earned the title "censor" for his willingness to instruct the public in morality. Bickerstaff describes the twofold duties in the office of Roman Censor:

The first part of it consisted in making frequent reviews of the people, in casting up their numbers, ranging them under their several tribes, disposing them into proper classes, and subdividing them into their respective centuries. . . . The second part of the Roman censor's office was to look into the manners of the people, and to check any growing luxury, whether in diet, dress, or building. (*Tatler* 162)

Addison added a third duty to the censor's office which is unspoken here but evident in many of his *Tatler*s. His Bickerstaff offers serious instruction in moral principles and religious beliefs. Although Steele commended these "noble discourses" in 1711, he may not have given his entire reaction to them until later years. Writing of Addison's *Tatler* pieces, Steele comments, "the elegance, purity, and correctness which appeared in his writings, were not so much my purpose," in a journal whose original intention was to rally and ridicule citizens into right behavior.[14] The "noble discourses" are Addison's distinctive contribution to the *Tatler*.

"Those Noble Discourses"

The noble discourses to which Steele refers form a small but important share of Addison's *Tatler*s and are unlike any piece that the originator attempted. In these numbers Addison treats religious attitudes or moral precepts too serious for standard *Tatler* treatment. *Tatler*s 119, 218, and 267 insist on the necessity for man to humbly acknowledge his creator. *Tatler*s 120 and 123 offer a vision of three stages of human life in which mankind is prompted by distinct motives: "Youth is devoted to lust, middle age to ambition, and old age to avarice." *Tatler*s 152, 154, and 156 summarize what men in different ages have believed about the immortality of the soul. Other *Tatler*s recommend the cultivation of specific moral habits. *Tatler* 146 advises acceptance of one's lot to avoid the gnawing misery of wishing to be someone else. *Tatler* 227 praises those who always look for good as noble minded while it brands those who stress faults as shallow minded.

Some of these noble discourses are straightforwardly didactic. Addison is in a humanistic tradition which emphasized literature's role in forming the ethical nature of mankind. The greatest writers are, in this view, the legislators of mankind. Addison's usual method is to discuss the topic in general terms and illustrate it with a retelling from classical literature. Bickerstaff proclaims, for example, that there is an alternative to London's debased taste for vulgar entertainments such as farce, which catches an audience by ridiculing and disgracing human nature:

I must confess, there is nothing that more pleases me, in all that I read in books, or see among mankind, than such passages as represent human nature in its proper dignity. As man is a creature made up of different extremes, he has something in him very great and very mean; a skillful artist may draw an excellent picture of him in either views. The finest authors of antiquity have taken him on the more advantageous side. They cultivate the natural grandeur of the soul, raise in her a generous ambition, feed her with hopes of immortality and perfection, and do all they can to widen the partition between the virtuous and the vicious, by making the difference between them as great as between gods and brutes. In short, it is impossible to read a page in Plato, Tully, and a thousand other ancient moralists, without being a greater and better man for it. (*Tatler* 108)

By moralists Addison does not mean just philosophers; he also means poets. Homer, Vergil, and Milton are as truthful commentators on human nature as Plato, Cicero, and England's own ancient, Francis Bacon. Addison is as apt to quote the first group as the second to illustrate a point. The series on the immortality of the soul instructs by retelling the adventures of Ulysses, Aeneas and Telemachus in the underworld. Alongside the "opinions of the greatest philosophers . . . it may likewise be worth while to consider, what men of the most exalted imaginations have thought of this matter" (*Tatler* 152). Addison's purpose in these *Tatler*s is little different from the purpose in his poetry: an epic story can adorn a prose precept just as heightened style or imagery can adorn a poem.

As an alternative to using classical literature to illustrate a lesson, Addison creates his own. His favorite device for enhancing the power of a precept to impress itself upon the reader is the dream vision. It could be used comically as in *Tatler*s 100 and 102 on Justice's reordering of the world, but it could also be employed for teaching seriously. The dream vision offers a revelation not easily apprehended by the conscious mind, an insight into the workings of the universe or a perspective of human life that is cosmic rather than mundane. To Addison, writing that contains the fabulous offers as pleasing and noble a picture of man as any straightforward account:

But since in history events are of a mixed nature, and often happen alike to the worthless and the deserving, insomuch that we frequently see a virtuous man dying in the midst of disappointments and calamities, and the vicious ending their days in prosperity and peace; I love to amuse myself with the accounts I meet with in fabulous histories and fictions: for in this kind of writings we have always the pleasure of seeing vice punished and virtue rewarded . . . so that inventions of this kind are like food and exercise to a good-natured disposition, which they please and gratify at the same time that they nourish and strengthen. The greater the affliction is in which we see our favourites in these relations engaged, the greater is the pleasure we take in seeing them relieved. (*Tatler* 117)

The dream visions were among Addison's most popular *Tatler*s with his contemporaries and are still not without a certain power.

Tatler 119 which presents the worlds upon worlds revealed by the microscope, *Tatler*s 120 and 123 which trace the three stages of human life, and *Tatler* 161 which extols the blessings of liberty all draw their power from Addison's skill in description. Even though the ideas are conventional enough in each paper, the selection of details invigorates these ordinary concepts. Each paper should be read in full, but a brief selection will instance Addison's descriptive skill.

Tatler 120 is Addison's version of a familiar image, that love is like a garden, "so mixed with roses and brambles, brakes and thorns and beds of flowers, rocky paths and pleasing grottos, that it was hard to say, whether it gave greater delight or perplexity to those who travelled it." On this stage men and women in the ritual of courtship conduct the attacks, retreats, and truces that punctuate the war between the sexes. Of a group of eager young men, the dreamer observes:

Some of their mistresses, who only seemed to retire for the sake of form and decency, led them into plantations that were disposed in regular walks; where, after they had wheeled about in some turns and windings, they suffered themselves to be overtaken, and gave their hands to those who pursued them. Others withdrew from their followers into little wildernesses, where there were so many paths interwoven with each other, in so much confusion and irregularity, that several of the lovers quitted the pursuit or broke their hearts in the chase. It was sometimes very odd to see a man pursuing a fine woman that was following another, whose eye was fixed upon a fourth, that had her own game in view in some other quarter of the Wilderness. (*Tatler* 120)

In *Tatler* 161 the subject is Liberty. Bickerstaff envisions a remote kingdom in the Alps where the goddess Liberty resides. The description of Liberty suggests the common assumptions of eighteenth-century Whigs rather than an original analysis by Addison. Monarchy sits at her right hand, Arts and Sciences, Plenty and Commerce attend her, and Tyranny and Licentiousness threaten her. What makes the vision imaginative is the enthusiastic depiction of the natural landscape as an emblem of polity. Wandering amid snow-capped mountains, the dreamer beholds an incredible sight:

I looked down from hence into a spacious plain, which was surrounded on all sides by this mound of hills, and which presented me with the most agreeable prospect I had ever seen. There was a greater variety of colours in the embroidery of the meadows, a more lively green in the leaves and grass, a brighter crystal in the streams, than what I ever met with in any other region. The light itself had something more shining and glorious in it than that of which the day is made in other places. (*Tatler* 161)

The account goes on to describe the allegorical figures that the narrator meets and his reaction to the pleasures of paradise. With less explicit political meaning or with more concentration on the narrator's experience, *Tatler* 161 would not be unlike a modern fantasy novel.

"Finest Strokes of Wit and Humour"

The genius of the *Tatler* papers resides in the fertile imagination of Steele and Addison. Though the whole series shows recurring topics and favorite techniques, there are few papers that are close imitations of others. The mark of the *Tatler* is variety. Three of Addison's best pieces, for instance, show his ability to transform familiar devices into something more.

*Tatler*s 153 and 157 belong to the group of allegorical papers which range people "under their several tribes, disposing them into proper classes." Other allegorical papers are noteworthy for the descriptive skill Addison bestows on familiar images or conventional thought. *Tatler*s 153 and 157 by contrast pay little attention to the moral and much attention to working out the original and imaginative allegory. The first paper treats conversations according to their similarities to musical instruments. Loud and noisy laughers who stand out in any crowd are the drums of society's orchestra. Quiet conversationalists who meet in small groups are the lutes. People who interject only occasional comments are the bass viols, while those who constantly return to the same topics are the trumpets. Incessant chatterers are like hunting-horns braying, braying in the forest; and tedious story tellers are big-winded bagpipes. After introducing each type,

Addison invites the reader to listen for these instruments in action all around him.

> If he has a mind to know where these several characters are to be met with, I could direct him to a whole club of drums; not to mention another of bagpipes, which I have before given some account of in my description of our nightly meetings in Sheer Lane. The lutes may often be met with in couples upon the banks of a crystal stream, or in the retreats of shady woods and flowery meadows; which for different reasons are likewise the great resort of your hunting horns. Bass-viols are frequently to be found over a glass of stale beer, and a pipe of tobacco; wheras those who set up for violins, seldom fail to make their appearance at Will's once every evening. You may meet with a trumpet anywhere on the other side of Charing Cross. (*Tatler* 153)

The second paper classifies types of female conversations and discovers flutes, a kit-fiddle, hornpipe, and harpsichord among others. It concludes with Bickerstaff 's friend recounting his love life in musical terms and finding that he has loved an entire consort. Upon which Bickerstaff issues a Table of Marriage showing which instruments, male and female, might play well together. Both pieces are virtuoso performances, carrying out the conceit as far as possible. The conceit is a challenge: just when the reader thinks the author has exhausted the similarities, he discovers one more, and then another.

Addison's development of imaginative techniques also shows itself in his handling of papers treating social characters. He shows a progressive movement away from the traditional character sketch which collected a body of qualities associated with a type of person. The descriptions of a Very Pretty Fellow and a Toast in *Tatler* 24 were already one step in a different direction. Addison here illustrated each type with two or three particular instances. Later papers show a further development: the type is embodied in one individualized example. This individual character takes on an identity. He is given a personal history, which often includes a place to live and a family to live with; he is given a voice to speak with. As Addison begins to pay attention to the details of the character and his environment, the moral becomes implicit rather than explicit. The character himself reveals the lesson or the narrator need only state it briefly. With the emphasis on narration of events and the depiction of character, Addison is not writing essays as much as short stories.

Tatler 155 is a delightful instance of this process of particularizing the traditional generalities of the character. The subject is the Political Upholsterer. Addison's opening description fixes him as a general type—the person who has a passion for political news—but also as a localized individual. He has a family, a history of up-and-down employment, and a favorite newspaper. The second paragraph brings the Political Upholsterer on stage for a scene created by a balanced mixture of description and dialogue.

This man and his affairs had been long out of mind, till about three days ago, as I was walking in St. James's Park, I heard somebody at a distance hemming after me: and who should it be but my old neighbour the upholsterer. I saw he was reduced to extreme poverty, by certain shabby superfluities in his dress; for, notwithstanding that it was a very sultry day for the time of year, he wore a loose great coat and a muff, with a long campaign-wig out of curl; to which he had added the ornament of a pair of black garters buckled under the knee. Upon his coming up to me, I was going to inquire into his present circumstances; but was prevented by his asking me, with a whisper, "Whether the last letters brought any accounts that one might rely upon from Bender?" I told him, "None that I heard of;" and asked him, "Whether he had yet married his eldest daughter?" He told me "No. But pray," says he, "tell me sincerely, what are your thoughts of the king of Sweden?" (for though his wife and children were starving, I found his chief concern at present was for this great monarch.) I told him, "that I looked upon him as one of the first heroes of the age." "But pray," says he, "do you think there is anything in the story of his wound?" and finding me surprised at the question, "Nay," says he, "I only propose it to you." I answered, "that I thought there was no reason to doubt it." "But why in the heel," says he, "more than in any other part of the body?" "Because," says I, "the bullet chanced to light there." (*Tatler* 155)

This account precedes a long disquisition by the Upholsterer on the political state of Northern Europe and a streetcorner discussion with other politically minded men. The narrator stands by quietly all the time and offers the moral only after he leaves the group behind: "This paper I design for the particular benefit of those worthy citizens who live more in a coffeehouse than in their shops, and whose thoughts are so taken up with the affairs of the allies, that they forget their customers."

Tatler 163 takes the predominance of the presentation over the moral one step further toward dramatization. After Isaac Bickerstaff gives a brief sketch of Ned Softly, a habitué of literary coffeehouses, the rest of this issue is a dialogue, without explicit moral point, between Isaac and Ned. Ned asks Isaac for comment about his poem, "To Mira on her Incomparable Poem." The poet insists on a line-by-line commentary, so that the censor is forced into vague and ambiguous comments to hide his real opinion. Here is their exchange about the second four-line verse of the poem:

"Let us now (says I) enter upon the second stanza. I find the first line is still a continuation of the metaphor.

'I fancy your song you sing.' "

"It is very right, (says he;) but pray observe the turn of words in those two lines. I was a whole hour in adjusting of them, and have still a doubt upon me, whether in the second line it should be, 'Your song you sing;' or, 'You sing your song.' You shall hear them both:"

'I fancy when your song you sing,

(Your song you sing with so much art,)'

or,

'I fancy when your song you sing,

(You sing your song with so much art.)' "

"Truly, (said I,) the turn is so natural either way, that you have made me almost giddy with it." "Dear Sir, (said he, grasping me by the hand,) you have a great deal of patience; but pray what do you think of the next verse?

'Your pen was plucked from Cupid's wing.' "

"Think! (says I,) I think you have made Cupid look like a little goose." "That was my meaning, (says he,) I think the ridicule is well enough hit off. But we now come to the last, which sums up the whole matter.

'For ah! it wounds me like his dart.'

"Pray, how do you like that *ah*! doth it not make a pretty figure in the place? *Ah*!—it looks as if I felt the dart, and cried out at being pricked with it.

'For ah! it wounds me like his dart.'

My friend Dick Easy (continued he) assured me, he would rather have written that *ah*! than to have been the author of the Aeneid." (*Tatler* 163)

The dialogue here is what the comedy of manners, whether in the plays of Congreve or the novels of Austen, achieves at its best. *Tatler* 158, about the pedantic scholar Tom Folio, and *Tatler* 165, about the false critic Sir Timothy Tittle, are similar in spirit and achievement to the Ned Softly paper.

Individually many of Addison's papers are small gems. But they glow a little brighter when one realizes how they are linked in the *Tatler* series. In a six-week period in 1710 (March 16–April 29), Addison composed fifteen *Tatler*s which display the whole range of his varied interests and devices. Looking at them in sequence, one sees why the *Tatler* kept and increased its readership. The range of tones from the serious to the playful and of techniques from expository essay to short story assured that each issue would bring some unexpected instruction or entertainment. In conjunction with Steele, the variations would be even greater. Though not forming one work, these fifteen pieces are Addison's most creative outburst thus far in his literary career.

Chapter Six
The *Spectator*

The *Spectator* is a great and unique work in English literature. If they had written nothing else, Joseph Addison and Richard Steele would deserve immortality for these 555 issues written over a period of almost two years. Their achievement is both contemporary and historical: they helped shape the culture of an age and in turn provided subsequent generations with an unforgettable portrait of that age. It is social as well as literary: they made journalism an art and they laid the foundations for the novel. All these topics critics and literary historians have explored.

But there is one achievement which has been undervalued. It belongs generally to both but particularly to Addison. The *Spectator* is a huge work which never lost its audience: it consistently maintained a level of intellectual sophistication and technical variety which brought readers back day after day. Neither Steele nor Addison ever ran out of things to say, but Addison especially seems to have found the means of stimulating continuous interest and to have discovered in that process resources of imagination and thought only dimly prefigured in his earlier writings. Addison fulfilled the dictum that Dr. Johnson laid down for all writers of periodical literature in *Rambler* 23: "He who endeavours to gain many readers, must try the various arts of invitation, essay every avenue of pleasure, and make frequent changes in his method of approach."[1]

"A Prodigious Run of Wit"

Three months after the *Tatler* ceased, Steele and Addison launched a new paper. Ironically, the *Spectator* had to compete with the numerous imitators of the *Tatler*. But compete it did and swept all other journals before it. The *Spectator* was everywhere in polite society. John Gay testifies, "Mean while the *Spectator*, whom we regard as our shelter from that Flood of False Wit which was breaking in upon us, is in every ones Hand, and a constant Topick for our Morning Conversation at Tea-Tables, and Coffee-Houses."[2] Circulation quickly reached the high level, for that time, of 3,000 with a possible readership of five or six persons for each copy. Produced six days a week, the *Spectator* ran for 555 issues between March 1, 1711, and December 6, 1712, surviving both imitators and a stamp tax that doubled its price.

Today literary historians and critics find the names *Tatler* and *Spectator* come trippingly together to the tongue, as easily as "Steele and Addison" or "Addison and Steele" come almost as one word. Their shares in the *Spectator* are exactly equal; each did 251 of the 555 issues.[3] Essays from these two periodicals are often anthologized together. Both our speaking and publishing habits suggest that in important ways we recognize a continuity between the *Tatler* and the *Spectator*. Together they form our most vivid storehouse of images and knowledge of life in early eighteenth-century London. The new journal reproduced many features of the old. Its fictional author-editor, like Isaac Bickerstaff, was a regular visitant of London's clubs and coffee-houses, a habitué of polite society. Like Isaac, too, he invited his readers to participate in the production of the paper by calling his attention to issues or responding to his judgments: "those who have a mind to correspond with me, may direct their letters *to the Spectator, at Mr. Buckley's* in *Little Britain*."[4] The *Spectator*, like the *Tatler*, presented in each issue a different perspective on London; each issue kept an open eye for the latest developments (a new play, the most recent fashion in ladies' wear, a new project) or for the eternal concerns (the pangs of love, the nature of friendship, the best manners).

But there is a crucial difference: the *Tatler* appeared thrice a week, but the *Spectator* appeared six times a week. The pressure of daily publication tested the resources of Steele and Addison as thinkers, journalists, and artists. What amazed contemporary readers and has impressed readers since is not that an issue appeared every day, but that a good issue appeared daily:

We had at first no manner of Notion, how a Diurnal Paper could be continu'd in the Spirit and Stile of our present *Spectators;* but to our no small Surprise, we find them rising upon us, and can only wonder from whence so Prodigious a Run of Wit and Learning can proceed; since some of our best Judges seem to think that they have hitherto, in general, outshone even the Esquires first *Tatlers.*[5]

Steele and Addison made "so Prodigious a Run of Wit" by the constant diversity of techniques. Some were carried over from the *Tatler:* the fictional editor-author who interacted with his society, the use of real and feigned letters from correspondents, the dream vision, the allegory, the character sketch of a social type. But the long run of the *Spectator* demanded and allowed the invention of new devices to provide the constant diversion which kept readers paper after paper: the *Spectator* club whose members could present the world from their own perspectives, the Oriental tale, the series discussion, the Saturday sermon, the hymn. Almost all innovations in technique were Addison's: Steele relied consistently on the device of the letter.[6] Steele, for instance, originated the club and the character of its most prominent members, but Addison did more to develop them. Steele's lack of technical experiment, in the long run, did not harm and may have enhanced the *Spectator.* Punctuated by Addison's diversity of technical experiment, Steele's pieces remain the constant, reassuring readers by the frequent return to familiar topics and procedures.

The "learning" of the *Spectator* to which Gay referred is also a distinctly Addisonian touch. Addison wrote the papers (*Spectators* 1, 10, 16, 124, 179, 221, 262, 435, 445, 476, and 542) in which Mr. Spectator explains his purpose and procedures. Like Isaac Bickerstaff, he is concerned with reforming the town, but his tone is that of an educator, not a satirist. Bickerstaff promised to "instruct persons of strong zeal and weak intellects" in "what to think." Mr. Spectator resolved to expand his audience's knowledge and stiffen its moral fiber:

And to the End that their Virtue and Discretion may not be short transient intermitting Starts of Thought, I have resolved to refresh their Memories from Day to Day, till I have recovered them out of that desparate State of Vice and Folly into which the Age is fallen. The Mind that lies fallow but a single Day, sprouts up in Follies that are only to be killed by a constant and assiduous Culture. It was said of *Socrates*, that he brought Philosophy down from Heaven, to inhabit among Men; and I shall be ambitious to have it said of me, that I have brought Philosophy out of Closets and Libraries, Schools and Colleges, to dwell in Clubs and Assemblies, at Tea-Tables, and in Coffee-Houses. (*Spectator* 10)

Though the *Spectator* does not ignore topics which made the *Tatler* a success (fashion, theatrical habits and trends, manners), it does add discussion of literary theory, philosophical and scientific concepts, ethical norms, and religious beliefs. Again Addison is primarily responsible. While Steele stuck to his perennial concerns of domestic life, love, and the theater, Addison, "who had read almost everything,"[7] acquainted his readers with the best classical authors and thinkers and the best modern ones. Besides Horace and Vergil he placed Scaliger and Ariosto, Montaigne and Pascal, Locke and Newton. He retailed this knowledge to the readers of the *Spectator,* acting as intermediary between the public and the world of learning. Addison's majority share in adding technical and topical variety—as well as his stylistic superiority—has led to one partisan assessment that "The *Spectator* survives in spite of Steele and because of Addison."[8]

Although separable in theory, wit and learning are one in the course of the *Spectator*. The author of these papers himself predicted that each quality shaped the other:

. . . I shall spare no Pains to make their Instruction agreeable, and their Diversion useful. For which Reasons I shall endeavor to enliven Morality with Wit, and to *T*emper Wit with Morality, that my Readers may, if possible, both Ways find their account in the Speculation of the Day. (*Spectator* 10)

The Various Arts of Invitation

So completely has Addison shaped Mr. Spectator in the character of a man who looks on without ever saying a word that some readers and critics have assumed the portrait is autobiographical. The assumption has colored Addison's reputation to the extent that anecdotes of his quietness in Parliament, where he supposedly watched business without daring a word, are readily believed. But Mr. Spectator's taciturnity is less autobiographical than artistic. It gives his character an appealing eccentricity, justifies his role as a giver of advice, and allows those whom Mr. Spectator meets to reveal themselves.

Whether called fools, humours characters, or originals, eccentrics have always delighted English readers. Eccentrics offer the world a seemingly distorted mirror which in fact often operates to smooth out the distortions in the world itself. Mr. Spectator describes himself in his first paper: he is so little given to conversation that during eight years at the university he scarcely said "the Quantity of an Hundred Words." And so he has continued in his life about town, visiting all the clubs of politicians, poets and merchants but never saying a word.

Thus I live in the World, rather as a Spectator of Mankind, than as one of the Species; by which means I have made myself a Speculative Statesman, Soldier, Merchant and Artisan, without ever meddling with any Practical Part in Life. I am very well versed in the Theory of an Husband, or a Father, and can discern the Errors in the Oeconomy, Business, and Diversion of others, better than those who are engaged in them; as Standers-by discover Blots, which are apt to escape those who are in the Game. (*Spectator* 1)

Unlike most taciturn men, Mr. Spectator is not a hater of mankind. In fact, he longs to share his thoughts and feelings: "When I consider how much I have seen, read, and heard, I begin to blame my Taciturnity; and since I have neither Time nor Inclination to communicate the Fulness of my Heart in Speech, I am resolved to do it in Writing; and to Print my self out, if possible before I die" (*Spectator* 1). This benevolence distinguishes Mr. Spectator from Isaac Bickerstaff; the former lacks the latter's aggressiveness and combativeness, which are requisite to the role of a censor.

Equally appealing is Mr. Spectator's willingness to talk to his readers. On occasion he asks their help. Mr. Spectator would appreciate the assistance of any reader "if he has met with any surprizing Story which he does not know how to tell, if he has discovered any epidemical Vice which has escaped my Observation, or has heard of any uncommon Virtue which he would desire to publish." On other occasions, he informs them about his process of composition: *Spectator* 124 points out the advantages of the brief essay for public instruction; *Spectator* 221 explains how he uses quotations from classical authors to give him a thought, provide an expression or supply an illustration. Often he keeps his readers informed on the progress of his plan to bring philosophy into the coffee-houses: *Spectator* 262 boasts its author's ability to instruct without "loose, obscene or immoral" thoughts or attacks upon the private lives of real people; *Spectator* 445 breaks the bad news to readers that a stamp tax will raise the price of subsequent issues. This familiarity capitalizes on the human desire to go behind the scenes. Though a good-humored, benevolent, and friendly narrator who always has his readers' best interests at heart,[9] Mr. Spectator can rail as well as advise and entertain to stir up certain readers:

There is another Set of Men that I must likewise lay a Claim to, whom I have lately called the Blanks of Society, as being altogether unfurnish'd with Ideas. . . I would earnestly entreat them not to stir out of their Chambers till they have read this Paper, that I will daily instill into them such sound and wholesome Sentiments, as shall have a good Effect on their Conversation for the ensuing twelve Hours. (*Spectator* 10)

Just as attractive and polite is the group of men with whom Mr. Spectator associates and the only company in which he has the courage to talk. Steele sketched the original characters of these intelligent, polite men: Sir Roger de Coverley, Sir Andrew Freeport, Captain Sentry, the Templar, Will Honeycomb, and the Clergyman. They represent the leisure class in its political and social contrasts: Tory landowner and Whig merchant, military veteran and fashionable man about town, the amoral playboy and the pious clergyman. The Spectator Club succeeds both because of Steele's first vivid description and because of development in later papers. Both Steele and Addison wrote several *Spectator*s purportedly contributed by club members. Of these the best by Addison are the Will Honeycomb papers (*Spectator*s 449, 511, 530). Reputed an inveterate rake and a wit upon female foibles, Will Honeycomb turns out just as agreeable to well-ordered society as the Clergyman or Sir Roger. *Spectator* 530 is a delightful expression of Will's personality; not even settling into a life as "a prudent Head of a Family" stifles the *joie de vivre* evident in his witty style.

The most fully developed and attractive of the club members is Roger de Coverley. He is as eccentric and benevolent as Mr. Spectator himself. (Not surprisingly, though Steele wrote the first sketch of him in *Spectator* 2, Addison wrote most of the papers about his character, as he did most of the papers on Mr. Spectator.) Though he dresses out of fashion, holds antiquated notions, and lacks learning, he is honest and charitable. Not only do the tenants and servants love this genial master but so do most Londoners. At the coffee-house

He had no sooner seated himself at the upper End of the high Table, but he called for a clean Pipe, a Paper of Tobacco, a Dish of Coffee, a Wax Candle, and the *Supplement,* with such an Air of Cheerfulness and Good-humor, that all the Boys in the Coffee-room (who seemed to take Pleasure in serving him) were at once employed on his several Errands, insomuch that no Body else could come at a Dish of Tea, till the Knight had got all his Conveniences about him. (*Spectator* 269)

Even subsequent readers felt the spell. One twentieth-century critic liked Sir Roger well enough to imagine the discovery of four new *Spectator*s about him.[10] Perhaps William Hazlitt said best what many readers then and now have thought about the Old Baronet and the other club members: "What old-fashioned friends they seem, and yet I am not tired of them, like so many other friends, nor they of me!"[11]

But neither Mr. Spectator himself nor his papers nor any of
his club members would have been half as appealing without the
stylistic resources of Addison and Steele. Two points should be
made about Addison's prose, which appear at first mutually ex-
clusive. That they appear contradictory, yet are in fact neatly
merged in the style of Addison, is the reason for the original
success and subsequent reputation of Addisonian prose.

The first point is that the style is conversational. The writer
is always aware that he is talking to someone; the reader is not
listening to a lecture; he is politely awaiting his turn to speak.
This conversational style is built on the rhythms of speech, takes
into account the reader's views, never exceeds his vocabulary, and
never raises its voice.[12]

The second point about this prose is that it is artistic. The easy
grace of Addison's prose appears natural but is, in fact, worked
at just as Castiglione's courtier practiced to make his skills unobtrusive. Addison once distinguished poetry from prose; the first
was adorned thought, the second unadorned. By his own definition Addison's prose is poetic. Addison is one of the first writers
to give English prose an artist's attention.

The primary qualities of Addison's style are balanced phrases,
familiar figures, and the juxtaposition of colloquial and learned
English.[13] Here is a passage about the itch for reading newspapers
which had recently afflicted the citizens of London, and Addison's
balm for turning the itch to account:

This general Curiosity has been raised and inflamed by our late Wars,
and, if rightly directed, might be of good use to a Person who has such
a Thirst awakened in him. Why should not a man, who takes Delight
in reading every thing that is new, apply himself to History, Travels,
and other Writings of the same kind, where he will find perpetual Fuel
for his Curiosity, and meet with much more Pleasure and Improvement,
than in these Papers of the Week? An honest Tradesman, who languishes
a whole Summer in expectation of a Battel, and perhaps is balked at
last, may here meet with half a dozen in a Day. He may read the News
of a whole Campain, in less time than he now bestows upon the Products
of any single Post. Fights, Conquests and Revolutions lie thick together.
The Reader's Curiosity is raised and satisfied every Moment, and his

Passions disappointed or gratified, without being detained in a State of Uncertainty from Day to Day, or lying at the Mercy of Sea and Wind. In short, the Mind is not here kept in a perpetual Gape after Knowledge, nor punished with that Eternal Thirst, which is the Portion of all our Modern News-mongers and Coffee-house Politicians. (*Spectator* 452)

The passage displays the attention (easy rather than strict) to parallel constructions of phrases, clauses and sentences. The metaphors of "thirst," "fuel," and the metonymy of "Sea and Wind" concretize the general contrast between newsreaders and book-readers. Other paired words like "languishes" and "balked" or "Gape after Knowledge" and "that Eternal Thirst" juxtapose Anglo-Saxon straightforwardness with suggestiveness and paraphrasis.

Like any prose style, Addison's has a limited range. It is too structured for spontaneous expression and too neat for powerful indictment. But Addison can modulate his style to fit a range of topics. Without such modulation Addison's *Spectator*s would tire quickly. In the following passage the same attention to balanced construction, contrasting vocabulary, and familiar images produces delightful humor:

I must here take notice, that *Rosalinda,* a Famous Whig Partizan, has most unfortunately a very beautiful Mole on the Tory part of her Forehead, which, being very conspicuous, has occasioned many Mistakes, and given an Handle to her Enemies to misrepresent her Face, as though it had Revolted from the Whig Interest. But whatever this natural Patch may seem to imitate, it is well known that her Notions of Government are still the same. This unlucky Mole however has misled several Coxcombs, and, like the hanging out of false Colours, made some of them Converse with *Rosalinda* in what they thought the Spirit of her Party, when on a sudden she has given them an unexpected Fire, that has sunk them all at once. If *Rosalinda* is unfortunate in her Mole, *Nigranilla* is as unhappy in a Pimple which forces her, against her Inclinations, to Patch on the Whig side. (*Spectator* 81)

Later in this chapter, a passage from *Spectator* 420 on the magnificence of the universe will show that Addison's style can speak enthusiastically as well as straightforwardly or humorously.

Without such a resourceful style Addison's *Spectator*s would not be such a varied achievement. The reasonableness, clarity, and confidence of the prose ensured that Mr. Spectator's voice would always be heard with respectful attention. His readers counted on his mediation between the boundless realms of knowledge and their own limited horizons, between the mysteries of the world and their own assumptions about it. Mr. Spectator could be trusted to find just the spot where two realms bounded and guide readers across the frontier. If the reader ever lagged behind, Mr. Spectator was sure to nudge him rather than kick him ahead.

"Frequent Changes in Method of Approach"

The contribution of two writers provided one source of variety in the *Spectator*. The varied personnel of the club provided a second. Alternations of audience, tone and method provide three more. Again Addison rather than Steele took the lead in providing diversity.

The Method of Balance. Unlike most of its periodical predecessors, the *Spectator* is conscious that its readership contains members of two sexes. Addison is equally confident about and attentive to the interests of men and of women. His "fair sex" papers on women's fashions, duties, and natures insured that he did not ignore half of his audience. A paper directed to one sex often brought in its wake a corresponding paper for the other. *Spectator* 198 cautioned "Salamanders," ladies who delight in dangerous flirtation, and *Spectator* 203 warned gentlemen to avoid becoming seducers. The deflation of male vanity in *Spectator* 275, "The Dissection of a Beau's Head," was balanced in the deflation of female vanity in *Spectator* 281, "The Dissection of a Coquette's Heart." Numerous papers include commentary to both sexes: *Spectator* 170 analyzes the causes of jealousy in men and women, and *Spectator* 57 humorously advises men to pay attention to their prime concern, fox-hunting, and ladies to theirs, fashion. Female fashion, however, is Addison's weak point when it comes to the fair sex papers. He never finds an equivalent issue on which to tease men, and there is a disproportionate attention to ladies' fads in the *Spectator*. Unfortunately Addison tries to have it both ways in regard to women: while teasing their attention to dress, he can think of little else to recommend to their attention except domesticity and maternity.

But there is a more important distinction Addison makes in his readership:

I may cast my Readers under two general Divisions, the *Mercurial* and the *Saturnine*. The first are the gay part of my Disciples, who require Speculations of Wit and Humor; the others are those of a more solemn and Sober Turn, who find no Pleasure but in Papers of Morality and sound Sense; the former call every thing that is Serious Stupid. The latter look upon every thing as Impertinent that is Ludicrous. (*Spectator* 179)

The different needs of each type of reader mean that no topic or presentation will satisfy them all. Yet Mr. Spectator intends both the Mercurial and the Saturnine to gather the same notions of manners, morals, and good taste. He reconciles his own purpose with his readers' interests by what can be called the "method of balance."

The method of balance insures that on all topics—the gentleman's code of conduct, the behavior of theater audiences, or good taste in literature—the *Spectator* brings all readers to similar notions. The method works by providing both a serious statement of principle which guides conduct or thinking, and a humorous depiction of violations of the principle through human weakness. For instance, *Spectator* 99 defines Honour as chastity in women and courage in men, and distinguishes real from romantic concepts. *Spectator*s 433 and 434, the fictitious histories of the "Republick of Males" and the "Republick of Females," make the same point comically by inverting traditional sex roles.

These balanced presentations of serious standards and comic deviations give the sober minded a clear statement and the witty a diverting change of perspective. But since neither type of reader knows which mode a given *Spectator* will be in, the Saturnine and Mercurial alike read each paper and are insensibly drawn closer in spirit:

As they neither of them know what I proceed upon, the Sprightly Reader, who takes up my Paper in order to be diverted, very often finds himself engaged unawares in a serious and profitable Course of Thinking; as on the contrary the Thoughtful Man, who perhaps may hope to find something Solid, and full of deep Reflection, is very often insensibly betrayed into a Fit of Mirth. (*Spectator* 179)

Addison's catering to opposite readers affects the form of his *Spectator*s. It is habit to refer to Addison's papers as essays but many are, in fact, little like what the modern reader understands by an essay, an expository treatment of an idea or an experience. Addison himself distinguishes two kinds of *Spectator*s:

Among my Daily-Papers, which I bestow on the Publick, there are some which are written with Regularity and Method, and others that run out into the Wilderness of those Compositions, which go by the name of *Essays*. As for the first, I have the whole Scheme of the Discourse in my Mind, before I set Pen to Paper. In the other kind of Writing, it is sufficient that I have several Thoughts of a Subject, without troubling myself to range them in such order, that they may seem to grow out of one another, and be disposed under the proper Heads. (*Spectator* 476)

The discourse appeals to the orderliness which the soberminded expect; the essay provides the freedom with which the witty delight to explore the vagaries of thought.

Addison's distinction between discourse and essay is readily observable. *Spectator* 177 which defines Good Nature is a discourse that could appear in a composition text as a model of structured writing. The introduction announces the thesis that there are four rules to Good Nature. Each of the next four paragraphs discusses one of the rules. The concluding paragraphs use examples to prove the thesis. The movement from topic to topic is controlled by formal transtions, "first," "for instance," and similar phrases.

The informally structured essay typified by *Spectator* 81 ("Party Patches") stands in contrast. Addison's account of party passion among the ladies begins with a long anecdote rather than a thesis. The anecdote which begins the piece is lengthened by two digressions; not until the sixth paragraph is the thesis announced.

Classical illustrations supporting the thesis that women have no place in politics conclude the essay.

Addison's method of balance owes certainly its spirit and perhaps its form to Horace, the Roman writer who best combined the age's ideals of urbanity, learning, and morality. Horace's *sermones* ("little talks") were probably as much a model for Mr. Spectator's papers as Montaigne, Seneca, Cicero, or Aristotle.[14] The *sermones* include satires which focus on follies or excesses in human behavior and epistles which offer encouragement to good conduct, good humor and good sense. All *sermones* display Horace's talent for the apt example or vivid illustration of the abstract principle; this same skill marks Addison's best *Spectator*s.

Whatever their source, discourses and essays are alternate paths to the same balanced center. The discourses fall into two groups, "Saturday sermons" and critical series. The former are so named because Addison usually published on Saturday a serious account of a moral virtue or a religious belief. As a group they are the least interesting of all Addison's papers; they offer only conventional wisdom uninspiringly illustrated by familiar anecdotes. The other discourses are the four series on literary subjects: tragedy, wit, *Paradise Lost,* and the Pleasures of the Imagination. Often the style and organization of these series are as uninspired as the Saturday sermons', but the thoughts are an important instance of the trend of critical ideas.

The so-called essays are Addison's most diverse and delightful collection of writings. Some are true essays, but others are short stories, visions, dreams, satiric sketches, and just unclassifiable pieces. Many of these essays use entertaining stories of situations as ways of infusing rather than preaching a point. In some cases the entertaining portion and the author's obvious delight in creating the details of that portion, eventually override the illustrative purpose for which it was first created. These pieces, in which Addison pushes aside the didactic to delight in the fanciful, form, with the critical series, his greatest achievement in the *Spectator.*

The Critical Series.   One way in which the *Spectator* taught, we have seen, is by returning to a topic several times at irregular intervals, with a different tone or method. Addison's recurring discussions of opera (*Spectator*s 5, 13, 18, 29, 31) illustrate this approach. A growing tendency in the journal is to devote a regular sequence of papers to one topic. It is uncertain how many of these series Addison had in mind when the *Spectator* began. On the one hand we have the testimony of Thomas Tickell that Addison's essays on literary topics grew from "little hints and minutes, which he from time to time collected, and ranged in order, moulded into the forms in which they now appear."[15] On the other hand, each series seems to have grown out of issues that earlier single papers had raised; each seems more ambitious than the last, and each reflects enlarged critical interests.

The first critical series, on tragedy (*Spectator*s 39, 40, 42, 44), seems to arise out of the attacks on the taste of London audiences for Italian opera. Addison promotes tragedy as a substitute for opera, equally enjoyable but more instructive: "As a perfect tragedy is the noblest production of human nature, so it is capable of giving the mind one of the most delightful and most improving entertainments" (*Spectator* 39). This and the succeeding essays on tragedy enumerate the criteria for plots, language, and stage effects. A tragic convention is justified or not according to ancient practice or theory. Thus most of Addison's "dramatick rules" are traditional, but there is one exception. His comments on poetical justice (the dictum that an author by the play's end must reward good characters and punish the bad ones) show a sophisticated understanding of literary rules. Critics like John Dennis and Thomas Rymer often judged as if following a rule alone made a good piece of literature. Addison, like the best Neoclassical critics, realizes there is always an appeal to human experience against the rules. Because life demonstrates that good men sometimes suffer while evildoers reap rewards, poetical justic must not tyrannize the dramatist or the play: "I do not therefore dispute against this way of writing tragedies but against the criticism that would establish this as the only method; and by that means would very much cramp the English tragedy, and perhaps give a wrong bent to the genius of our writers" (*Spectator* 40).

This quote expresses what is often implicit and occasionally explicit in Addison's criticism: the interest in how future writers will be molded and guided. Addison's judgments of past writers and literature seems aimed at pointing writers toward the best models. The spirit is apparent in the next series of essays upon false and true wit (*Spectators* 58 through 63). The series seems to grow from both immediate and underlying interests. The immediate interest is the attempt to synthesize ideas on the nature of wit and humor raised in *Spectators* 35 and 47; the underlying interest is Mr. Spectator's purpose of providing, by his own papers, a true entertainment for an audience whose contentment with inferior forms of literature he frequently laments.

Forms of False Wit are essentially verbal tricks—the pun or acrostic—in which the resemblance of words masquerades as thought. True Wit on the other hand consists of a resemblance of ideas which delights and surprises a reader with an insight into human experience: "Thus when a poet tells us, the bosom of his mistress is as white as snow, there is no wit in the comparison; but when he adds, with a sigh, that it is as cold too, then it grows into wit" (*Spectator* 62). Addison's lecture in essays 58 through 62 is concluded in the dream vision of *Spectator* 63 with Mr. Spectator's pseudoepic descent into the "Region of False Wit" which allegorizes all the theoretical conclusions of the previous papers. It offers the delightful congruence of judgment and image. For example, Addison sees puns as "another set of merry people engaged at a diversion, in which the whole jest was to mistake one person for another" (*Spectator* 63).

Addison's standard for discriminating true and false wit is partly ancient authority and partly his own experience of what has the more powerful effect on the imagination of the audience. This dual perspective simultaneously makes Addison old-fashioned and forward-looking as a critic. His twin perspectives are evident as well in Addison's next sequence of papers on literature.

This more ambitious critical series is the seventeen papers written on *Paradise Lost* (*Spectators* 267, 273, 279, 285, 297, 303, 309, 315, 321, 327, 333, 339, 345, 351, 357, 363, 369). One essay appeared each Saturday between January 5 and May

3, 1712. The Saturday appearance is significant—Saturday's essay was always Addison's lay sermon in preparation for Sunday. Mr. Bickerstaff's habit of explaining important religious ideas through the use of literature obviously passed down to Mr. Spectator. Although Addison focuses on the literary features of the poem, he is attentive as well to the religious lessons. The central doctrine is the consequences of Adam and Eve's disobedience; and "besides this great moral, which may be looked upon as the soul of the fable, there are an infinity of undermorals which are to be drawn from the several parts of the poem and which make this work more useful and instructive than any other poem in any language" (*Spectator* 369).

Both the topic of Milton's great epic and Addison's discussion show the writer's closeness to his audience. On the one hand, *Paradise Lost* had become widely read in the early eighteenth century: it was available in several formats, from an expensive "coffee table" edition to a handy pocket-sized one.[16] Addison was capitalizing on popular interest and attempting to give it guidance and direction by pointing out the work's poetic merits. On the other hand, the series apparently outgrew its original designs because of reader interest. Addison ends his last paper (*Spectator* 369) on *Paradise Lost* by attributing the length of his analysis to "the kind reception" and "the uncommon demand of his readers."

The sequence of the seventeen essays shows how they just "growed." The first four essays (267, 273, 279, 285) analyze Milton's poem as a conventional epic by comparing its fable, actors, sentiments, and language to those of the *Iliad* and the *Aeneid*. Addison finds Milton in all cases the equal of Homer and Vergil. After a pause in the sequence to discuss what a critic ought to do (*Spectator* 291), Addison in the next two papers (*Spectators* 297 and 303) mentions some of the weaknesses as well as beauties in the poem. Narrowing down his discussion of what Milton does well, the next essay (*Spectator* 309) treats "the great justness and delicacy" in the characterizations of the underworld figures, Mammon, Beelzebub, and Satan, which are the topics of Books I and II. The following paper (*Spectator* 315) praises

Milton's description in Book III of heaven and its inhabitants, so well done that they fill the mind "with thoughts of devotion."

The last nine essays (321, 327, 333, 339, 345, 351, 357, 363, 369) show continued focusing down. First each essay discusses one book of *Paradise Lost,* Books IV through XII. After Addison completes the general discussion by *Spectator* 303, he quotes the poem more and more frequently in order to discuss particular passages. Such passage-by-passage, line-by-line analysis, which can grow tedious to the general reader, is softened by the gradualness with which it is introduced and by the spacing out of the essays. It is ultimately the heart of Addison's purpose: "In short, I have endeavored to particularize those innumerable kinds of beauty, which are essential to poetry, and which may be met with in the works of this great author" (*Spectator* 369).

Milton is great for the same reasons Addison cited for Vergil's greatness in the "Essay on the Georgics." Milton is a poet preeminent for ornamenting precepts in the delightful garb of poetry. Discussing how Milton's God and angels are made to speak on theological topics, Addison writes:

He has represented all the abstruse Doctrines of Predestination, Free-Will, and Grace, as also the great point of Incarnation and Redemption, (which naturally grow up in a Poem that treats of the Fall of Man,) with great Energy of Expression, and in a clearer and stronger Light than I ever met with in any other Writer. As these Points are dry in themselves to the generality of Readers, the concise and clear manner in which he has treated them, is very much to be admired, as is likewise that particular Art which he has made use of in the interspersing of all those Graces of Poetry, which the subject was capable of receiving. (*Spectator* 315)

Since Addison defines poetry as ornamented thought, Milton's other great quality is his power of description. Addison consistently praises passages of *Paradise Lost* as "beautiful," "surprising" or "elevated." He never defines explicitly the power of description in *Paradise Lost,* but rather clusters a series of important adjectives around this aspect of Milton's art. Description means here more than it did in the "Essay on *Vergil's Georgics*": the ability to make the written account of a thing as vivid to the senses as the object itself.

Milton's achievement lies in the sweep of his poetry, its ability to invoke the vast scale of the universe and of eternity in the account of the cosmic warfare between God and Satan. It lies too in surprising and bold ideas like the attribution of artillery to the rebellious angles. It lies as well in the use of fresh, powerful images or similes, and in the maintenance of a formal and dignified tone unbroken by colloquial or idiomatic language. Milton's art also raises the reader's passions by involving him in the greatest and yet most fundamental human drama: disobedience, punishment, and sin.

One word in Addison's vocabulary sums up Milton's passages, which are simultaneously "beautiful, surprizing, and elevated." That word is sublime. Addison never defines the term, but reserves it as the highest adjective of praise. Addison's use of "sublime" derives from Longinus' treatise "On the Sublime," one of the most famous classical pieces of literary criticism. The sources of the sublime listed by Longinus are precisely the characteristics Addison finds in Milton's verse: "a Boldness and Grandeur in the Thoughts . . . a skillful Application of Figures . . . a noble and graceful manner of expression . . . Composition of the Periods in all possible Dignity and Grandeur."[17]

What finally does "sublime" mean? It means the power of the kind that a poem like *Paradise Lost* exercises over its readers. The sublime is whatever is

grand and lofty, which the more we consider, the greater Ideas we conceive of it; whose Force we cannot possibly withstand; which immediately sinks deep, and makes such Impressions on the Mind as cannot be easily worn out or effaced.[18]

Its effect goes beyond giving mere literary pleasure. Since Longinus was a Platonist, he sees literature as a path to the experience of divinity.[19] The effect of the sublime is to ennoble men, to make them more virtuous and more conscious of their immortality. No wonder Addison placed his discussion of *Paradise Lost* on Saturday. By pointing out where Milton was "grand and lofty"

Addison put his readers under the influence of those passages which "make such Impressions on the Mind as cannot be easily worn out or effaced." The papers on *Paradise Lost* are a development on earlier *Tatler* papers in which summaries of literary works help explicate notions of virtue and doctrine. Here literature is more subtly employed on behalf of morality: the consideration of the poem's Paradise exposes the reader to the sublime impact of its truths about God's ways to man. It is a fulfillment of Addison's earlier dictum: "For here the Mind, which is always delighted with its own discoveries, only takes the hint from the Poet, and seems to work out the rest by the strength of her own faculties."

Addison's final series of *Spectator* papers is explicitly conclusive, the last stage in Mr. Spectator's plan "to banish this Gothick taste" (*Spectator* 437) for epigrams, puns, and strained metaphors, in favor of literature that betters or enlarges the mind of the reader. *Spectator*s 411–21 on the Pleasures of the Imagination attempt to understand how literature gives pleasure. Number 409, which introduces Addison's plan to publish eleven consecutive papers on this topic, announces his intention to articulate the principles which have underlain his previous particular judgments on literature. Like the other critical series these essays are based on notes and drafts written earlier.[20]

The theory which *Spectator*s 411–21 develop is the most ambitious critical effort in any of Addison's essays and the most methodical exposition of the idea which he had put forward in his undergraduate writings: that vivid description is the most important effect of poetry. Although issued in eleven parts, the theory is rigidly schematic. To explain the pleasures of the imagination "such as arise from visible object," *Spectator* 411 distinguishes primary pleasures "which entirely proceed from such objects, when they are not before the eyes." Subsequent papers develop the analysis of each pleasure according to its sources, cause, and types.

Spectator 412 finds three sources of primary pleasure: the greatness ("the largeness of a whole view, considered as an entire piece"), the novelty, and the beauty of objects themselves. *Spec-

tator 413 finds the final cause of primary pleasures in God's threefold design that man seek Him, pursue knowledge, and propagate his species. The next two papers explain types of primary pleasures, those arising from works of Nature and those from works of architecture.

Spectator 416 assigns the same three sources for secondary pleasures but notes that the sense of beauty proceeds here from "that action of the mind which compares" the original object with a description of it. The same paper locates the final cause of secondary pleasures in God's will "to quicken and encourage us in our searches after truth" and classifies their four types: statuary, painting, music and literature. Each of the last five papers (*Spectators* 417–21) discusses one facet of literature's descriptive power: it is a product of the innate imaginative genius of great writers; it works "with violence" upon a reader's emotion; it explains the appeal of such different works as romances ("the fairy-way of writing") and scientific tracts of the New Philosophy; and it enables the mind to grasp abstract ideas.

One important aspect of the series which a summary does not reveal is how synthetic Addison's ideas are. He is intellectually indebted to many writers and philosophers. His basic premise, that sight is the main source of the mind's ideas, comes from John Locke's *Essay on Human Understanding* (1690).[21] He was indebted to Thomas Hobbes, Aristotle, Le Bossu, and others for ideas on the novelty as a source of imaginative pleasure.[22] For literary examples and judgments, Addison drew heavily on Dryden.[23] The interest in Longinus he shared with the French critic Boileau and John Dennis.

To credit a writer with a synthesis is sometimes damnation with faint praise. It may suggest that he is incapable of deep thought. But to evaluate Addison's synthesis it is important to consider why he sought to synthesize such thinkers, so diverse in time and in philosophical approach. Addison's era was a time of intellectual as well as political ferment; his papers on the imagination seek to reconcile classical humanistic culture with modern scientific culture. It was a reconciliation evident in Addison's intellectual life since his days at Oxford where he preferred the new philosophy at the same time he studied Roman poets. Although not explicitly, Addison attempts to resolve questions raised by the controversy of the Ancients and Moderns: is not Nature itself a more profitable object of study than poetry or any other art? Does not a mechanistic-materialistic view of man's nature obviate the need for a personal Creator of the universe? Is not the scientific method of observation and experimentation superior to the rule-making of critics and philosophers?

Addison's reconciliation of these opposing attitudes hinges on the assumption that the works of God (Nature) and the works of man (Art) fully please only as they resemble one another: "If the products of Nature rise in value, according as they more or less resemble those of art, we may be sure that artificial works receive a greater advantage from their resemblance of such as are natural" (*Spectator* 414). Nature by itself readily produces examples of greatness and novelty, but art more consistently supplies regularity and proportion. The combination is essential to give the fullest pleasure the imagination can experience.

Because the combination of art and nature underlies aesthetic pleasure, Addison can build the understanding of one on the reader's appreciation of the other. Addison's evidence for man's delight in the primary pleasures of color, shape, and motion is literary evidence, his own Latin verse (*Spectator* 412) or that of Horace and Vergil (*Spectator* 413). Conversely to distinguish the different pleasures one receives from reading Homer and Vergil, it is necessary to use similes from nature.

Reading the *Iliad* is like travelling through a country uninhabited, where the fancy is entertained with a thousand Savage Prospects of vast Deserts, wide uncultivated Marshes, huge Forests, mis-shapen Rocks and Precipices. On the contrary, the *Aeneid* is like a well-ordered Garden, where it is impossible to find out any Part unadorned, or to cast our Eyes upon a single Spot, that does not produce some beautiful Plant or Flower. (*Spectator* 417)

If nature and art, then, are linked in the pleasures of the imagination and intertwined in its understanding, those who study need not choose between the ancients and the moderns because, wherever they start, both conclude in the same place. Old writers and new writers perfect Nature. Each stimulates the reader's imagination by presenting Nature in a way not readily seen. The poet may combine the qualities of different seasons in one passage or the flowers of different climates in one description, all to show off Nature's greatness, strangeness or beauty. "The authors of the new philosophy" do no less when they communicate through their work science instead of poetry, but the telescope and microscope's revelations about an unknown and unseen Nature have the same effect on the imagination:

Nothing is more pleasant to the fancy, than to enlarge it self, by Degrees, in its contemplation of the various Proportions which its several Objects bear to each other, when it compares the Body of Man to the Bulk of the whole Earth, the Earth to the Circle it describes round the Sun, that Circle to the Sphere of the fixt stars, the sphere of the fixt Stars to the Circuit of the whole Creation, the whole Creation it self to the Infinite Space that is every where diffused about it; or when the Imagination works downward, and considers the Bulk of a Human Body, in respect of an Animal, a hundred times less than a Mite, the particular limbs of such an animal, the different springs which activate the Limbs, the Spirits which set these springs a going, and the proportionable Minuteness of these several Parts before they have arrived at their full Growth and Perfection. (*Spectator* 420)

The ancient and modern poets, then, are linked by an ability to affect the imagination. They are likewise linked by a purpose, the "embellishment of good sense . . . sets off all writings in general" (*Spectator* 421). This is the familiar Addisonian concept of poetry, enunciated in the "Dissertatio" and the "Essay on Vergil's *Georgics*." By appealing to the imagination the poet at the same time insinuates precepts into the understanding. But in these papers Addison gives this talent its greatest sanction: "It has something in it like creation" (*Spectator* 421). The poet, in fact, is the image of the Divine Creator, who has created the delightful things of the universe in order to lead man to Himself.[24] The Creator embellishes the works of nature as a poet embellishes his precepts, to lead the mind insensibly to the discovery of prin-

ciples: "what reason can we assign for their exciting in us many
of those ideas which are different from anything that exists in
the objects themselves, (for such are light and color) were it not
to add supernumerary ornaments to the universe, and make it
more agreeable to the imagination?" He embellishes Nature with
greatness to give a suggestion of his own infinite nature, with
the new or uncommon to inspire man's search after knowledge,
with beauty to insure that "all creatures might be tempted to
multiply their kind, and fill the world, with inhabitants" (*Spectator* 413).

Such are the intellectual reconciliations abstractly. But they
must in turn be reconciled in a person—the reader of the *Spectator*.
Spectator 411 suggests the ideal of "a man of polite imagination"
who is able to appreciate the sensibility which the upcoming
essays will depict. His appreciation will put him equally at ease
in a museum or on a country estate:

He can converse with a Picture, and find an agreeable Companion in
a Statue. He meets with a secret Refreshment in a Description, and
often feels a greater Satisfaction in the Prospects of Fields and Meadow,
than another does in the Possession. . . . So that he looks upon the
World, as it were, in another Light, and discovers in it a Multitude
of Charms, that conceal themselves from the generality of Mankind.

It will also develop and preserve his moral nature: "A Man should
endeavour, therefore, to make the Sphere of his innocent Pleasures
as wide as possible, that he may retire into them with safety,
and find in them such a Satisfaction as a wise Man would not
blush to take. Of this Nature are those of the Imagination."
Finally it encourages *"mens sana in corpore sano"*:

Delightful Scenes, whether in Nature, Painting, or Poetry, have a
kindly Influence on the Body, as well as the Mind, and not only serve
to clear and brighten the Imagination, but are able to disperse Grief
and Melancholly, and to set the Animal Spirits in pleasing and agreeable
Motions.

Thus the papers on the Pleasures of the Imagination offer another way for Mr. Spectator to achieve his goal of molding the hearts and heads of his readers.

"Essay Every Avenue of Pleasure"

To the methods of varying topics and treatment already discussed, Addison adds one more. When exposition and discourse fail he writes imaginative creations of his own. As we have seen Addison often turns to ancient and modern literature for poetic passages and tales which illustrate the truth of a social comment, a moral principle or a religious belief. Most of the time he is content to copy or repeat passages from classic writers, folklore, or collections of Oriental tales. Usually these passages are short and merely illustrative. On several occasions, though, Addison is not content with such use; he writes his own poems, fanciful sketches, and stories which come to dominate rather than support the idea of the essay.

Poetry. In the late summer and fall of 1712, Addison attempted "divine poetry," his first original English verse since "The Campaign." Five of his Saturday sermons (*Spectators* 441, 453, 465, 489, 513) contain original hymns. He seems to have taken an interest in hymns for several reasons besides the normal *Spectator* ones. His father had written devotional poems; hymn writing had become a popular topic after recent reforms allowing hymns as replacements for Psalms at liturgical functions; they were a useful and varied means of instruction. Addison's five poems, usually referred to as "the *Spectator* hymns," are "The Lord my Pasture shall prepare," "When all thy mercies O, my God," "The Spacious Firmament on high," "How are thy servants blest, O Lord!" and "When Rising from the bed of Death." Addison had praised the ballad form for its sincere and simple emotion; this interest may have influenced the clear expression of feeling that characterizes his hymns.[25]

Each hymn is used to exemplify the thesis of the essay in which it is included; each takes up anywhere from the last fourth to the last half of the essay. The topic of *Spectator* 441, for instance, is man as a creature "subject every Moment to the greatest Calamities and Misfortunes." Man's only remedy in his predicament is "a firm Reliance on him [God] for the Blessings and Conveniences of Life, and an Habitual Trust in him for Deliverance out of all such Dangers and Difficulties as may befall us."

The essay concludes by citing the biblical David as the exemplar of the reliant attitude. In the twenty-third Psalm David sings,

> The Lord my Pasture shall prepare,
> And feed me with a Shepherd's Care.

Thus, Addison's hymn illustrates his thesis. In each *Spectator* the hymn reinforces the moral point by vivid example.

But the hymn seems to do more than just illustrate the thesis. Analogous to the hymn sung between the sermon and Communion in the Anglican liturgy or to the songs sung on St. Cecilia's Day, Addison's hymns aim to intensify the thesis of the essay, to raise rational understanding to spiritual insight. Addison concludes: "When all thy Mercies, O my God," for example, with two stanzas that suggest the transporting emotion of song, recalling the imagery of harmony and melody of his "Song" (1693) but casting the emphasis more effectively on the singer himself:

> When Nature fails, and Day and Night
> Divide thy Works no more,
> My Ever-grateful Heart, O Lord,
> Thy Mercy shall adore.
>
> Through all Eternity to Thee
> A joyful Song I'll raise,
> For oh! Eternity's too short
> To utter all thy Praise.

The emphasis on the hymn as edification accounts for the common characteristics of what might be called the personal hymns of *Spectator*s 441, 453, 489, and 513. The diction of these hymns is simple: common words, mostly of one or two syllables. The syntax is simple: each line is composed of a single sentence, clause or phrase so that the reader's understanding is never complicated by the author's style. The structure of each hymn is as simple and direct as the language. The four stanzas of "The Lord my Pasture shall prepare" trace the passage from life through death to paradise. "When all thy Mercies, O my God," tucks nine narrative stanzas between introductory and concluding stanzas which set up and summarize the theme. The stanzas trace man's passage from infancy to youth to middle age to old age and show the kind of reliance appropriate for each stage. "When rising from the bed of Death" balances three stanzas of doubt and worry—the sinner's concern with "How shall I appear" at the judgment—with three stanzas of comfort and hope—the sinner is not alone.

These poems are noteworthy for emphasizing the feeling of the individual soul at the same time they employ the common imagery of Christianity: the shepherd and his sheep, the pilgrimage through life, the faith in Christ's atonement for sin. They are the only expressions of Christian piety in Addison's corpus. The presence of the individual experience within the group experience is best exemplified by the description of the storm in *Spectator* 489. Here the narrator experiences his spiritual serenity amid the general consternation of passengers and the upheaval of the sea. Aware of the external events, the hymn yet focuses on the interior experience that is the result of them.

> Confusion dwelt in ev'ry Face,
>   And Fear in ev'ry Heart;
> When Waves on Waves, and Gulphs in Gulphs,
>   O'er came the Pilot's Art.
>
> Yet then from all my Griefs, O Lord,
>   Thy Mercy set me free,
> Whilst in the Confidence of Pray'r
>   My Soul took hold on Thee;
>
> For tho' in dreadful Whirles we hung
>   High on the broken Wave,
> I knew Thou wert not slow to Hear,
>   Nor Impotent to Save.

The hymn of *Spectator* 465, "The Spacious Firmament on high," is unlike the other four. The diction is more formal, the vocabulary more abstract, the syntax more complicated. The three-stanza structure adapts the classical patern of strophe, antistrophe, and epode to the Psalmist's proclamation that the heavens declare the glory of God. Its rational piety is Addison's typical religious attitude.

Addison's hymns, sometimes shortened, became standard in many eighteenth-, nineteenth- and twentieth-century collections. "The Spacious Firmament on High" has appealed most, but the more personally expressive hymns appealed to the same congregations that sang the hymns of Isaac Watts. Even today Addison's hymns maintain a reputation. "The Lord my Pasture shall prepare" is still considered the best transcription of the twenty-third Psalm.[26] Addison's divine songs instance his ability to cultivate a small field of literary endeavor.

Fiction.   Addison frequently retold or invented fictional anecdotes to adorn a moral. Usually his storytelling is short and straightforward, always pointed to its purpose and just detailed enough to serve as clear example. Addison used fiction of all popular modes: allegories, visions, Oriental tales, love stories, and character sketches.[27] But as the hymns sometimes dominate the discourses they ornament, several papers show Addison moving away from the tale as illustrating device, toward delight in dramatization, plot and character portrayal. Of all the storytelling in the *Spectator* three pieces stand out: "Theodosius and Constantia" (164), "The Vision of Mirzah" (159), and the Roger de Coverley papers (especially 106, 110, 112, 122, 131, 269, 329, 335, 383).

One type of popular story at which Addison tried his hand successfully is the tale of lovers' woes. Both Steele and Addison frequently used such stories to illustrate ideas or principles about family life. These domestic apologues appear in *Spectator*s 123 and 215 as examples of what should and should not be done in the education of young people. *Spectator* 164 is Addison's most extended such story, in which concern for character and feeling takes precedence over the didactic purpose.

The story of Theodosius and Constantia is Addison's sentimental version of the well-known medieval love story of Eloise
and Abelard. The courtship of the lovers is interrupted by Constantia's father, who seeks to marry his daughter to a rich heir;
he is concerned about a profitable match, not his daughter's
feelings. Broken-hearted by the plans of marriage, Theodosius
disappears. Convinced her lover is dead, Constantia blames herself
for his death and insists on retiring to a convent instead of mar-
rying. Theodosius, thinking Constantia has wed, becomes a
priest: coincidence brings the lovers together when Constantia
comes to "Father Francis" for confession. They recognize each
other, but because religious vows now prevent marriage, they
agree to correspond by letter. Only death ends their extraordinary
correspondence. Theodosius and Constantia both die in the plague
and are buried side by side.

"The Vision of Mirzah" combines the dream vision and the
Oriental tale. *Spectator* 159, like most of Addison's contributions,
aims to give advice, but this one attempts to do so unobtrusively
by casting its theme—that earthly life is a dangerous passage or
pilgrimage to a better, heavenly existence—in the form of a
manuscript which Mr. Spectator has found. The manuscript contains the first vision of Mirzah, a Moslem contemplating the
vanity of human life as part of his holyday's meditation. Lulled
by a shepherd's melodies, Mirzah meets the Genius (we would
say "genie" today) of that lonely spot who transforms the normal
landscape into a scene encapsulating all human existence. Mirzah
sees a valley with a sea sweeping through it: the valley is the
Vale of Misery; the sea is the tide of eternity. A bridge of seventy
arches crosses the sea, a bridge crowded with the stupendous
multitudes of humanity. Mirzah sees that many do not cross all
seventy arches of the bridge, for not all men live out a full life.
By accident or by the malice of spirits many plunge into the sea
below. Both ends of the bridge—the origin and the end of human
life—are covered with cloud, for no man sees whence he came
or where he is going. The reader, like Mirzah, learns of the vanity
of human existence by watching this drama unfold.

But if the reader is concentrating on constructing the unobtrusive moral, the writer is devoting his attention to constructing an engrossing and vivid narrative. For instance, Mirzah is granted a vision of what lies behind the clouds which cover the end of life:

[It] . . . appeared to me a vast Ocean planted with innumerable Islands, that were covered with Fruits and Flowers, and interwoven with a thousand little shining Seas that ran among them. I could see Persons dressed in glorious Habits, with Garlands upon their Heads, passing among the Trees, lying down by the Sides of Fountains, or resting on Beds of Flowers; and could hear a confused Harmony of singing Birds, falling Waters, humane Voices, and musical Instruments.

When Mirzah asks the Genius for a glimpse behind the clouds at the other end of the bridge, he discovers the genius vanished and the vision gone:

I turned about to address my self to him a second time, but I found that he had left me; I then turned again to the Vision which I had been so long contemplating, but instead of the rolling Tide, the arched Bridge, and the happy Islands, I saw nothing but the long hollow Valley of *Bagdat,* with Oxen Sheep, and Camels, grazing upon the Sides of it.

The balanced triplets of the final clause, so tangible and so antithetical, snaps the dream at once.

The most ambitious fictional effort in the *Spectator* is what have come to be called "the De Coverley papers." Although Steele's original sketch had given Sir Roger a history connecting him to actual places and people, he exists from the first as a representative of a gentry class and of a Tory viewpoint. His character offered a flexible device by which to accomplish the twin aims of diversion and instruction. But in the course of the thirty-three issues that make up the De Coverley papers, Sir Roger grew beyond his first use. He takes on the rounded existence of a great character from the drama or the novel. Eventually he is depicted for the sake of depiction, not for other purposes.

Sir Roger as a vehicle of instruction has several clear uses. Representing the viewpoint of traditionally Tory country squires, he makes the *Spectator* broad in its social and political views. As a resident of the country, he enables Mr. Spectator to leave London and present new subjects and new perspectives for his observations. For example, Mr. Spectator's visit to Sir Roger's estate and observation of his poultry lead to speculations about the ways that the life of animals proves the existence of a Divine Providence (*Spectators* 120 and 121). As a governor of an estate Sir Roger can provide instruction in the code of the gentleman: generosity and ease with servants and tenants (*Spectators* 107 and 117), cooperation with and support of the clergy (*Spectator* 112), necessity of proper recreation and exercise to balance learning (*Spectators* 115 and 116).

But Steele's opening sketch also provides for the development of Sir Roger as a character in his own right. The outline provided of his life allows future essays to develop episodes about his past. *Spectator* 109 takes us through the De Coverley family portrait gallery to observe the fashions and manners of a bygone age in which Sir Roger still lives. In *Spectator* 113 Sir Roger recounts his affair with the "perverse Widow" who threw him over. *Spectator* 122 dramatizes how Sir Roger earns his tenants' and neighbors' esteem by settling their arguments; *Spectator* 130 shows him having his fortune told by one gypsy and his pocket picked by another—both with equal equanimity.

Addison and Steele in most of the De Coverley essays have a similar attitude toward Sir Roger, an attitude implicit in the opening description that he is "rather beloved than esteemed." In many ways Sir Roger is a figure of fun. He is somewhat of a Dickensian character: warm-hearted, naive, loved, old-fashioned, and somewhat ill at ease or out of place when he is not in the simpler rural setting of his home. He is a model for domestic virtue, but he is not the model for the man about town. Since Sir Roger represents the predominantly Tory class of landed men, the political implication is clearly that while he is a fine individual he and his class are not fit to govern a whole nation. For the glory of the De Coverleys is all in the past.[28] Steele sums up the double attitude after Sir Roger relates how an ancestor narrowly escaped being killed in the Civil War (1641–1646), "for, said he, he was sent out of the Field upon a private Message the Day before the Battel of Worcester." The remark leads Mr. Spectator to muse, "The Whim of narrowly escaping, by having been within a Day of Danger, with other Matters above-mentioned, mixed with good Sense, left me at a Loss whether I was more delighted with my Friend's Wisdom or Simplicity" (*Spectator* 109).

Although Steele develops more of Sir Roger's character at first while Addison uses his estate as a soapbox from which to preach domestic precepts, it is Addison who eventually takes over the lovable squire. After his frequent appearances in Numbers 106 through 130, Sir Roger disappears for one hundred and thirty-nine *Spectators*. When he does return in *Spectator* 269, Addison handles him differently.

This attitude prevails in the remaining *Spectators* (329, 383, and 517) by Addison which treat Sir Roger. Each of them emphasizes the scene within which the character is displayed; there are no lessons to be learned nor any precepts to be decorated. In *Spectator* 329 the professed topic is a visit to the national shrine of Westminster where England's heroes are buried; but receiving equal attention is the narrative introduction. Mr. Spectator comes to Sir Roger's lodging; the knight offers him a glass of "Widow *Trueby's* Water." Mr. Spectator drinks it and winces while Sir Roger apologizes for the foul taste but defends the water's medicinal qualities. The preparations for departure continue as the friends talk of Widow Trueby's concoction:

I could have wished indeed that he had acquainted me with the Vertues of it sooner; but it was too late to complain, and I knew what he had done was out of Good-will. Sir *Roger* told me further, that he looked upon it to be very good for a Man whilst he staid in Town to keep off Infection, and that he got together a quantity of it upon the first News of the Sickness being at Dantzick: When of a sudden turning short to one of his Servants standing behind him, he bid him call an Hackney-Coach, and take care it was an elderly Man that drove it.

He then resumed his Discourse upon Mrs. *Trueby's* Water, telling me that the Widow *Trueby* was one who did more Good than all the Doctors and Apothecaries in the Country.

In developing aspects of Sir Roger's character and illuminating more of his romantic past, at the same time that it narrates how Mr. Spectator and Sir Roger got ready for their visit and adds observations on country life, the passage is marvelously active.

The growth of Sir Roger from an occasion for instruction to a character delightful for himself reaches its epitome in *Spectator* 517, which announces his death. There is nothing extraordinary about the manner of Sir Roger's death or about the manner which it is announced: he died in his bed of some unspecified ailment and that fact is related simply in the butler's letter, accompanied by one of Sir Roger's favorite books, to Mr. Spectator. The emotion generated by the news of Sir Roger's death is deftly handled by Addison, by attention to one detail and one member's reaction. The detail is given in the postscript to the letter:

This letter, notwithstanding the poor Butler's manner of writing it, gave us such an Idea of our good old Friend, that upon the reading of it there was not a dry Eye in the Club. Sir *Andrew* opening the Book found it to be a Collection of the Acts of Parliament. There was in particular the Act of Uniformity, with some Passages in it marked by Sir *Roger's* own hand. Sir *Andrew* found that they related to two or three Points, which he had disputed with Sir Roger the last time he appeared at the Club. Sir *Andrew*, who would have been merry at such an Incident on another Occasion, at the sight of the old Man's Handwriting burst into Tears, and put the Book into his Pocket.

But the effect of the De Coverley papers is not only sentimental. The attention to the contemporary setting, the interaction of socially distinctive characters, and the depiction of personality influenced two developing genres concerned with these same issues: the novel and the biography.[29] If not for the irregularity of Sir Roger's appearances, Addison and Steele rather than Richardson might have gained literary fame for the first novel: "Here, for the first time, are the methods and subjects of the modern novel; all that is wanting is a greater unity and continuity of scheme to make the 'Coverley Papers' in the *Spectator* a serial novel of a very high order."[30]

Sketches. Addison wrote a number of fictional pieces which defy easy classification, but which are among his most original and delightful *Spectator*s. Many of them use a distinctive device so that Mr. Spectator hardly ever seems to repeat himself. Usually the purpose of these surprising fictions is to give a new perspective on London life, manners, and morals that shows how ridiculous, vain, or vicious some practice is. The meaning of the sketch is to be found in the antithesis between style and content, rather than in plot or character. No doubt Addison intends the reader to discover on his own the precept behind the antithesis.

One of the important features of these sketches is to bring opinions, albeit fictional opinions, to support Mr. Spectator's judgments on London's manners, tastes or morals. *Spectator* 50 purports to be An American Indian's report to his countrymen on the curious customs of Englishmen. Like Mr. Spectator he finds certain habits of dress absurd, behavior in church the opposite of expected, and political partisanship rampant. *Spectator* 317 uses an insider's perspective rather than an outsider's to show how one can waste attention and time on mere habits without care to the serious improvement of the heart or mind. Here is one day's entry in the journal of a Sober Citizen:

MONDAY

Eight a Clock. I put on my Cloaths and walked into the Parlour.

Nine a clock, ditto. Tied my Knee-strings, and washed my Hands.

Hours Ten, Eleven and Twelve. Smoaked three Pipes of *Virginia.* Read the *Supplement* and *Daily Courant.* Things go ill in the North. Mr. *Nisby's* Opinion thereupon.

One a Clock in the Afternoon. Chid *Ralph* for mislaying my Tobacco-Box.

Two a Clock. Sat down to Dinner. *Mem.* Too many Plumbs, and no Sewet.

From Three to Four. Took my Afternoon's Nap.

From Four to Six. Walked into the Fields. Wind, S.S.E.

From Six to Ten. At the Club. Mr. *Nisby's* Opinion about the Peace.

Ten a Clock. Went to Bed, slept sound.

Another feature is that these fictional sketches often combine a familiar technique with a contemporary interest. *Spectator*s 275 and 281 combine the dream vision and modern science as Mr. Spectator attends the dissection of a beau's head and a coquette's heart. The perfectly objective tone, scientific terminology, and implied moral judgment achieve a delicately balanced ridicule.

We did not find anything remarkable in the Eye saving only, that the *Musculi Amatorii*, or as we may translate it into *English*, the *Ogling Muscles*, were very much worn and decayed with use; whereas on the contrary, the *Elevator* or the Muscle which turns the Eye towards Heaven, did not appear to have been used at all. (*Spectator* 275)
Nor must I here omit an Experiment one of the Company assured us he himself had made with this Liquor, which he found in great quantity about the Heart of a Coquet whom he had formerly dissected. He affirmed to us, that he had actually enclosed it in a small Tube made after the manner of a Weather-Glass; but that instead of acquainting him with the Variations of the Atmosphere, it showed him the Qualities of those Persons who entered the Room where it stood. He affirmed also that it rose at the Approach of a Plume of Feathers, an embroidered Coat, or a Pair of fringed Gloves; and that it fell as soon as an ill-shaped Periwig, a clumsy pair of Shoes, or an unfashionable coat came into his House. (*Spectator* 281)

Other sketches which rely on delightful inventions are *Spectator* 343, which is the supposed firsthand account of the adventures of Pugg, a monkey, written for his mistress, and *Spectator* 361, which relates the history of cat-calls. Each has its point which is meant to seep into the reader's mind through the delight in ornament rather than through force of reason. Addison's reputation as a humorist securely rests on these sketches.

Chapter Seven
Later Periodical Prose

After the heyday of Mr. Spectator, Addison contributed to six more periodicals before his death. Three of his contributions (to the *Lover*, the *Reader*, and the *Old Whig*) are eminently forgettable. The other three (the *Guardian*, a revived *Spectator*, and the *Freeholder*) are worth remembering.

The *Lover* (February to May 1714) and the *Reader* (April to May 1714) were Richard Steele projects, for each of which Addison wrote two papers. *Lovers* 10 and 39 are familiar ideas in new garb: the latest fashion to be ridiculed is the passion for china dishes; the latest writer to be plumped is Eustace Budgell. *Readers* 3 and 4 hardly bother with a fresh approach; they virtually reprint parts of the *Whig-Examiner*. The *Old Whig* (March to April 1719) is unimpressive for another reason. It defended the Peerage Bill against attacks from Richard Steele's paper, the *Plebeian*. The spectacle of old partners trading sneers and innuendoes is distasteful. Both papers lack either the wit of Isaac Bickerstaff or the good sense of Mr. Spectator.

The *Guardian*, the revised *Spectator*, and the *Freeholder*, however, demonstrate that Addison had learned a good deal about the arts of keeping an audience through a mixture of serious and entertaining subjects. In many papers Addison draws successfully on the resources—discourse, essay, tale, letter or sketch—which made the *Tatler* and *Spectator* successful. On the whole, the subsequent journals lack a stimulating framework or context like those of the first ventures. The *Guardian* narrows intellectual and cultural horizons and strengthens domestic topics. The revised *Spectator*, in the crisis year 1714, has all the morality but less of the wit of the first *Spectator*. The *Freeholder* is locked to the events and issues of the rebellion in 1715–1716 against George I.

The *Guardian*

Richard Steele began the *Guardian* on March 12, 1713. Like the *Spectator* it appeared six times a week, but it did not begin as a cooperative effort. Addison contributed only two of the first ninety-six issues. In July, however, Richard Steele concentrated his attention on getting elected to Parliament and turned the *Guardian* over to Addison. Half of the remaining essays are Addison's. His first contributions were of a miscellaneous nature: a paper urging theater-goers to support a benefit performance for the playwright Tom D'Urfey, an essay on coinage, a satire on political informers. But once regular contributions began, Addison fell in with Steele's plan. As the *Spectator* takes for its province the world of coffee-houses and clubs, the *Guardian* attends to the household. Like other periodicals edited by Steele, the *Guardian* ended for a reason that had less to do with its success and more to do with its format. The last issue appeared on October 1, 1713, because Steele founded the *Englishman*, a political paper devoted to insuring that a Hanover, not a Stuart, followed Queen Anne to the throne.

For the *Guardian* Richard Steele created the author-editor Nestor Ironsides. Like his "renowned kinsmen and predecessors" Bickerstaff and Spectator, Nestor knows the coffee-houses and tea-tables of London. Nestor's real interests, however, are the concerns of the family, especially the Lizard family, whom he serves as guardian. The Lizard family, whose problems set up a frame for many *Guardian* essays, is the most innovative device in the new periodical.[1] Less aggressive than Bickerstaff and less eccentric than Spectator, Nestor Ironsides is a steady fellow whose integrity, wisdom, and good humor the reader is inclined to trust.

Addison molds most of his *Guardian* essays to fit Steele's focus. While maintaining the variety of subjects characteristic of the earlier periodicals (English climate in *Guardian* 102, criticisms of Dryden's plays in 110, the designs of Providence in 117), Addison points most of his contributions toward domestic topics and issues. The concern for literary taste so evident in the *Spectator* is minor here: only six of Addison's contributions discuss poetry or drama. The emphasis of the *Spectator* on moral and religious subjects is subdued: only five papers treat virtues or beliefs as abstract concepts. The *Tatler's* sense of social participation is weaker in the *Guardian*: only seven issues treat characters or institutions of the town.

Rather the focus is on the family, its relationships, duties and entertainments. Addison presents wives too fond of gambling, daughters in need of education, heads of family too proud of their lineage, fathers inattentive to their children's needs, newlyweds uncertain of their new state, and lovers despairing of winning a beloved. What creates variety in the presentation of these topics is the use of different tones appropriate to the circumstances. These tones may be characterized as outrage, exposition, and ridicule.

Outrage is reserved for the pain of destroyed domestic harmony. Nestor's description of the moral and physical degeneration of wives addicted to gambling in *Guardian* 120 or the letter in *Guardian* 123 from a working-class mother to the aristocratic seducer of her daughter are expressions of pain rare in Addison's writings. In the latter issue the mother ends her long recrimination with this outburst:

Wretchedness is now become my everlasting portion! Your crime, my lord, will draw perdition even upon my head. I may not sue for forgiveness of my own failings and misdeeds, for I never can forgive yours; but shall curse you with my dying breath, and at the last tremendous day shall hold forth in my arms my much wronged child, and call aloud for vengeance on her defiler.[2]

On issues less serious but still essential to domestic peace, Addison maintains the straightforward and reasoned tone of the "Saturday sermons" in the *Spectator*. *Guardian*s 111 and 159, for instance, discuss the necessity of education for young gentlemen and young gentlewomen. The first essay offers a mixture of practical and idealistic reasons: education is an adornment for old age, an ideal for even Alexander the Great, who preferred knowledge over conquest, and a source of wealth and fame. The second essay argues by the example of the fate of Miss Betty, who refused the embellishments of learning as a young girl and later had to become a servant when her father lost his fortune. In most papers on domestic virtues, Addison describes and recommends the proper mode of conduct by either anecdotes from classical history or by fictional stories about modern characters. Almost all the illustrative tales in the *Guardian* are short and obvious. The delight in storytelling itself, or the contentment with implying the moral, which characterizes many of the best *Spectators*, is absent in the *Guardian* recommendations of virtue.

In the matter of ridiculing the foibles of fashions and manners, Nestor's humor complements the preaching of clergymen: "while they are employed in extirpating mortal sins, and crimes of higher nature, I should be glad to rally the world out of indecencies and venial transgressions" (*Guardian* 116). Therefore, Nestor rallies such venial sins as the absurdities of masquerades (*Guardian* 154), the hazards of courtship (*Guardian* 97), and affectation in wedding clothes (*Guardian* 113). The best papers in this group are those which take an imaginative view of old problems. *Guardian* 112 teases the excesses and inconsistencies of lovers from a novel perspective: what would happen if people could fly. When a fictional correspondent boasts to Nestor that he is learning to fly, the Guardian points out the dangers of this new human talent:

It would fill the world with innumerable immoralities. . . . You should have a couple of lovers make a midnight assignation upon the top of the monument, and see the cupola of St. Paul's covered with both sexes like the outside of a pigeon-house. Nothing would be more frequent than to see a beau flying in at a garret window, or a gallant giving chase to his mistress, like a hawk after a lark. There would be no walking in a shady wood without springing a covey of toasts. The poor husband could not dream what was doing over his head. (*Guardian* 112)

Nestor's most sustained campaign in fashion is directed against low-cut dresses, or, as the *Guardian* calls it, "the exorbitant growth of the female chest." Decolletage is the central concern of a half-dozen papers. The topic is first raised by Addison's favorite device for commenting on manners: the casual report of a recently observed phenomenon.

I observed this as I was sitting the other day by a famous she visitant at my Lady Lizard's, when accidentally, as I was looking upon her face, letting my sight fall into her bosom, I was surprized with beauties which I never before discovered, and do not know where my eye would have run, if I had not immediately checked it. (*Guardian* 100)

Successive comments try to maintain a moderate tone, stressing the immodesty of the fashion without sounding puritanical. On the one hand, Nestor offers the conventional wisdom that such temptation ought not to be put in the path of all young men, that sexual allurement is the province of the unmarried, and that covered "beauties" allure just as effectively by mystery.

On the other hand, the standard bearer of morality becomes a figure of fun. *Guardian* 109 presents reactions to Ironsides's pleas for modesty. Several young ladies reprove him. One pointedly remarks that women "do not dress for an old fellow, who cannot see them without a pair of spectacles" and another insulted miss complains that she "is forced to return a pair of stays which were made in the extremity of the fashion, that she might not be thought to encourage peeping." The support that Nestor receives comes from the wrong quarters, for the wrong motives. "Half a dozen superannuated beauties" thank him that now their "antiquated necks" will not have to compete with younger, fuller, and smoother bosoms. More support comes from a young lady whose complexion does not show up well in the current fashions, and from the Pope, who has issued fierce proclamations against overexposure of the female breast. Another supporter is glad that Nestor has intervened to stop the trend toward fashionable nakedness, which would soon have deprived all women of the stays, girdles, and other unseen enhancers of shapeliness.

The undercutting of Nestor's authority places his campaign halfway between moral imperative and fuddy-duddy thinking. The reader is left to decide to which side a balanced judgment should lean. The final letter from a reader on the subject of low necklines shows that though fashion has not led to outright immorality, it has set conjugal relationships on the ear. A merchant in Turkey writes,

> In short, sir, the tables are now quite turned upon me. Instead of being acquainted with her person more than other men, I have now the least share of it. When she is at home, she is continually muffled up, and concealed in mobs, morning gowns, and handkerchiefs; but strips every afternoon to appear in public. For aught I can find, when she has thrown aside half her clothes, she begins to think herself half dressed. (*Guardian* 134)

Eventually readers' experiences will confirm the moralist's position.

Addison's share of *Guardian* essays reuse but do not add to the variety of techniques which characterize his *Tatler* and *Spectator* essays: letters, stories, sketches, and discourses. He does attempt one variation on the employment of letters. Nestor announces to his readers his intention to construct a lion's head statue outside Button's into whose mouth may be dropped a request for advice or a commentary upon manners. Nestor promises to report these letters once a week as the "roarings of the lion" in support of piety, justice, and virtue.

The device of the lion's head endures several months. It is a logical culmination of Addison and Steele's effort to project their daily papers as cooperative activities between author and reader. The lion's head offers anyone the chance to be a Guardian. Better yet, the device allows Addison to introduce some variety of topics. *Guardian* 71 describes the origin of such lion heads at Venice, "curiously wrought in marble with mouths gaping in a most enormous manner. Those who have a mind to give the state any private intelligence of what passes in the city, put their hands into the mouth of one of these lions, and conveys into it a paper." *Guardian* 98 describes Nestor's plan to construct one at the coffee-house. *Guardian* 114 announces that construction has been completed and the mouth is ready to be fed. *Guardian*s 118 and 124 reveal the first assistant guardians. Leontilla Figleaf, a mantilla maker, offers to report the news from the dressing room, and a leonine-looking scholar offers to roar from Cambridge. A tourist writes to assure everyone that, yes, truly, the lion's head is a sight to behold. In *Guardian* 140 an astrologer casts the lion's horoscope.

As useful as the lion's head is, it essentially is only a letter-box; and letters, delightful as many are, cannot carry the burden of interest. Addison's reliance on letters, real or feigned, is symptomatic of a larger failure. The *Guardian*s are an intellectual and artistic step below the *Spectator*. The falling short is evident in the celebrations of nature, the literary criticism, and the use of fiction. *Guardian* 103 repeats, for instance, the theme of *Spectator* 465 that the heavens proclaim the glory of God. In this case, however, the occasion for the essay is a fireworks display, which although magnificent in its way yet pales beside Nature's fireworks in a comet, which lead man to form "exalted notions of infinite wisdom and power." The contrast of human and natural pyrotechnics does not make the point with the impact of "The Spacious Firmament on High." Mr. Spectator, inspired to poetry, is more convincing than Nestor Ironsides, moved to explicit statement. Similarly, the literary criticism of *Guardian*s 115, 119, and 122 fails to match the *Spectator* essays on wit, *Paradise Lost,* or the Pleasures of the Imagination. The *Guardian* merely retells how the Italian critic Strada represented ancient poets in a pageant; the *Spectator* essays contain a synthesis and a defense of literary values. The fictional achievement is likewise less. The best Oriental tale of *Guardian* 167 is full of romantic intrigue, a Romeo and Juliet story dressed in Arabian garb. A father administers a drug which induces a deathlike sleep in order to save his daughter and her lover from a lusty and jealous king. Through this ruse the lovers escape to the country, where they live until the king dies. The story moves quickly and pleases because right wins out; however, it is not quite as compact and pointed as the Oriental tales of the *Spectator* and certainly lacks the greatness or distinctive combination of elements that marked the "Vision of Mirzah."

Addison's *Guardian*s are generally below the quality of his *Spectator*s, but there are exceptions. Simon Softly's expensive but futile courtship of a widow (*Guardian* 97) is delightful humor, and the confusions likely at a masquerade (*Guardian* 154) are handled with a sense of farce. *Guardian*s 153, 156, and 157 present a fable from the new philosophy; the image of an anthill as a microcosm of human society rests on scientific observation. *Guardian* 67 interestingly adapts the methods of fictional characterization to a real purpose.

Perhaps no other paper shows off the virtues of Addison's style so well. The paper employs the persuasion of art for a practical purpose: to encourage readers to attend a performance of *The Plotting Sisters*. In 1713 its author, Thomas D'Urfey, was an aging, poor, but able poet; he must have reminded Addison of Dryden in 1693. Addison composes a moving portrait of D'Urfey by adapting the techniques which made Sir Roger de Coverley such an endearing fellow. Reversing the normal sequence in which a real person vouches for a fictional one, Addison makes the fictional character vouch for the actual person. Nestor Ironsides reports touching scenes he personally witnessed: "I myself remember King Charles the Second leaning on Tom D'Urfey's shoulder more than once, and humming over a song with him." Addison creates a fictional world about D'Urfey as he created a real one about Sir Roger. The stereotyped characters of D'Urfey's songs come alive as flesh-and-blood people:

Should the very individuals he has celebrated make their appearance together, they would be sufficient to fill the playhouse. Pretty Peg of Windsor, Gilian of Croyden, with Dolly and Molly, and Tommy and Johnny, with many other to be met with in the musical miscellanies, entitled "Pills to purge Melancholy," would make a good benefit night.

The portrait ends by skillfully balancing a summary of the poet's achievements with a detail of the man's humanity:

I might here mention several other merits in my friend; as his enriching our language with a multitude of rhymes, and bringing words together, that, without his good offices, would never have been acquainted with one another, so long as it had been a tongue. But I must not omit that my old friend angles for a trout the best of any man in England. *May* flies come in late this season, or I myself should, before now, have had a trout of his hooking. (*Guardian* 67)

The Continuation of the *Spectator*

On June 18, 1714, Addison gave up his long association with Steele. For the first time since the *Whig-Examiner* he undertook a periodical without the assistance of his old partner. To capitalize on past success he called the new journal (published Monday, Wednesday, and Friday) the *Spectator*; to stress the continuity he numbered the first issue 556. His purpose is also that of the original: a nonpolitical commentary on the state of the nation. Addison abandoned the political paper war that Steele could not help:

As these Politicians of both Sides have already worked the Nation into a most unnatural Ferment, I shall be so far from endeavouring to raise it to a greater Height, that, on the contrary, it shall be the chief Tendency of my Papers to inspire my Countrymen with a mutual Good-will and Benevolence. Whatever Faults either Party may be guilty of, they are rather inflamed than cured by those Reproaches which they cast upon one another. The most likely Method of rectifying any Man's Conduct, is, by recommending to him the Principles of Truth and Honour, Religion and Virtue; and so long as he acts with an Eye to these Principles, whatever Party he is of, he cannot fail of being a good *Englishman,* and a Lover of his Country.[3]

The continuation of the *Spectator* never regained the original's popularity, however. The new essays simply do not have the variety of the original series. For one thing, Mr. Spectator is "quite another Man to what I used to be." His former reticence is gone; he returns to print a talkative man. Thanks to long hours of practice reading aloud in his room, chatting with ladies at tableside, and entering coffee-house arguments with local wits, Mr. Spectator is now a talker. Now he is like almost every other Londoner of consequence; his eccentricity is gone.

Other factors hurt the new journal. In the first issue Mr. Spectator promises a new club will be formed, but it never is. The writers assisting Addison in producing issues—Thomas Tickell, Eustace Budgell, and others—lacked the humor, fervor, and talent of Steele. Addison's own contributions are not as varied. Only nine of his twenty-five essays mix "wit with morality."

He employs predominantly the Saturday-sermon style; infrequently he employs the diverting and entertaining techniques of allegory, dream vision, Oriental tale, and dramatized scene. Overall, the new *Spectator* is more serious-minded.

Addison's contributions stopped after *Spectator* 600. He had become increasingly occupied with his duties as Secretary to the Regency, the council assigned to insure George's smooth accession to the throne. Thomas Tickell assumed the dominant role in the *Spectator*, but it was not a financial success. It ceased once and for all with *Spectator* 635 on December 20, 1714.

The main theme of the continuation is the Man of Integrity. Probably influenced by the success of his tragedy *Cato* and afraid of the instability inherent in political crisis, Addison focuses most of his attention on the qualities that make a man stand firm during troubled times and that allow him to speak plainly. The second issue of the new *Spectator* (557) begins with a description of the Roman senator Cato, renowned for his adherence to truth and principle in the most trying times. His steadfastness, when "a little softened and qualified by the Rules of Conversation and Good Breeding," provides a model for behavior to which both Whigs and Tories should look. Addison quotes Bishop Tillotson on how this steadfastness and honest mode of expression combine to create the qualities of "the old English Plainness and Sincerity, that generous Integrity of Nature, and Honesty of Disposition which always argues true Greatness of Mind, and is usually accompanied with undaunted Courage and Resolution." Here is John Bull Catoized.

To make the point that contemporaries do not have the virtue of "Plainness and Sincerity"—and at the same time direct attention away from political controversy—Addison uses as his example a letter supposedly written by the Javanese ambassador to England. It is one of the best anecdotal illustrations Addison ever wrote, but is unfortunately untypical of the material in the continuation. The ambassador describes to his lord several *faux-pas* he has committed because he expects plain speaking and takes literally the overstated and careless expressions of some Englishmen:

I lodged the first Week at the House of one who desired me *to think my self at home, and to consider his House as my own.* Accordingly, I the next Morning began to knock down one of the Walls of it, in order to let in the fresh Air, and had packed up some of the Household-Goods, of which I intended to have made thee a Present: But the false Varlet no sooner saw me falling to work, but he sent Word to desire me to give over, for that he would have no such Doings in his House. I had not been long in this Nation, before I was told by one for whom I had asked a certain Favour from the chief of the King's Servants, whom they here call the Lord-Treasurer, That I had *eternally obliged him.* I was so surprized at his Gratitude, that I could not forbear saying, What Service is there which one Man can do for another, that can oblige him to all Eternity! However I only asked him for my Reward, that he would lend me his eldest Daughter during my Stay in this Country; but I quickly found that he was as treacherous as the rest of his Countrymen. (*Spectator* 557)

Except for three papers which stereotype widows as husband-abusers more interested in estates than emotional commitment (*Spectator*s 561, 584, 585), Addison's remaining twenty-two contributions revolve around these twin concepts of the ideal of the Man of Integrity and the necessity for "old *English* Plainness and Sincerity."

Addison develops neither concept in as systematic a fashion as he developed his criticism on *Paradise Lost* or the Pleasures of the Imagination. He never gives a strict definition of the Man of Integrity or of the plain-speaker, but he does cluster qualities around each by returning to these themes constantly. For the most part, following the method of balance used in the earlier *Spectator*s, Addison develops the Man of Integrity by positive suggestions seriously given. The Plain-speaker is described by ridiculing deviations from the norm.

What are the qualities of the Man of Integrity? He finds a middle path between the frivolity of a merry temperament and the dourness of a serious one (*Spectator*s 576, 598). He has learned to be content with his lot in life (558, 559, 574), to carry out the duties of his station (583), and to treat others with humanity and compassion (594). He avoids the fashionable vices of adultery (579) and drunkenness (569). His integrity is founded on a right idea of a divine being (571, 580), a recognition of the Creator's gifts (565, 571), and a sense of responsibility for his immortal soul (600). Such prudential wisdom would sound hollow if always presented in the same tone. In these essays, as in the original *Spectator*, Addison's style ranges from the humorous to the fanciful to the poetic as the subject demands.

Moderation, humor, and respect are the marks of the Man of Integrity. Lapses in these qualities immediately manifest themselves in language. Mr. Spectator observes that too often writers love "I" more than any word to stress their singularity (*Spectator* 562). The "itch of writing" turns the printing press into a means to "scatter Prejudice and Ignorance through a People" (*Spectator* 582). The scandal sheet caters to the human weakness for hearing badly of others (*Spectator* 567). The bad critic reveals himself by the propensity to find faults instead of virtues (*Spectator* 592).

As in the earlier *Spectator* and *Guardian* essays, imitation, parody and ridicule are Addison's techniques for pointing out deviations from the ideal. The frequency and imagination of such papers in the revived *Spectator*, however, fall short of the achievement in the previous journals.

The *Freeholder*

Addison's *Freeholder*, fifty-five issues between December 23, 1715, and June 29, 1716, was written during the Jacobite rebellion in Scotland, which attempted to place the pretender James III on the throne. In some ways it was a return to the journalism of the *Whig-Examiner*. Both were Addison's sole productions, both expressed the government's viewpoint at a moment of crisis, both kept readers up to date on events and answered the printed propaganda of the opposing party. The *Freeholder* waged propaganda war on the home front to consolidate the successes of the military on the battlefield: "While many of my gallant countrymen are employed in pursuing rebels half discomfited through the consciousness of their guilt, I shall labor to improve those victories to the good of my fellow subjects; by carrying on our successes over the minds of men, and by reconciling them to the cause of their king, their country, and their religion."[4]

No one essay lists all of Addison's reasons why Englishmen ought to reconcile themselves to king, nation, and Church. Rather, the reasons are spread out over the fifty-five issues. Addison's position is that Englishmen, under the Hanoverian monarchy, enjoy political liberty and economic prosperity. Thus the title of the *Freeholder,* one who possesses the minimum property qualification in order to vote, appeals to the common denominator of Englishmen from yeoman to lord. The institutions, persons, and policies of the current balanced and Protestant government, Addison consistently argues, offer the best chance of maintaining that prosperity and freedom. *Freeholder* 2 describes George I as a king who will abide by the laws of the constitution, love his adopted country, and possess the personal valor and heroism to ensure England's freedom from foreign enemies. *Freeholder* 4 advises that Protestant subjects will not flourish under a Catholic king. *Freeholder* 10 argues that England's mixed and balanced constitution—in which the king, the aristocrats, and the people share power through the court, the House of Lords and the House of Commons—is a better guarantee of liberty than trusting the absolutist, even if beneficent, claims of a Stuart. *Freeholder* 12 pictures rebellion as the destroyer of civil society rather than the creator. *Freeholder* 16 lauds the administration's restrained use of extraordinary powers such as the suspension of *habeas corpus* while *Freeholder* 20 praises the limited taxation implemented only for the duration of the revolt. *Freeholder* 31 acclaims the leniency with which government has treated captured rebels. *Freeholders* 41 and 42 stress that England's prosperity depends on her trade which only George I and the Whigs are firm in supporting. *Freeholder* 50 sums up that nations are advanced permanently by reasonable government, not by sword of rebellion.

Although these essays primarily intend to show the political wisdom of maintaining the status quo, they also demonstrate how much Addison has matured as a periodical journalist. The *Freeholder* has been called, incisively, a "political *Spectator.*" If the purpose of the *Spectator* was to enliven morality with wit, and temper wit with morality, then the *Freeholder* enlivens the Hanovers with wit and tempers disaffection with morality. Addison employs over his fifty-five numbers a range of topics and techniques similar to that in previous journals. Political argument alternates with thoughts on education, the virtues, the world of women, and the plight of writers. Logical exposition gives way on occasion to allegory, Oriental tale, character sketch, and pseudomemoir.

The combination of political purpose and *Spectator* variety was doubtless deliberate. While taking the rebellion seriously, the *Freeholder*'s combination of politics and entertainment makes clear that the threat is manageable. The world of the Englishman is not going to change drastically or suddenly; there is ample time to pay attention to the ladies, to note the best authors, and to have a laugh at the rebels' expense. The *Freeholders* attempt to soothe rather than exacerbate political feelings, to offer a reasonable compromise to opponents, to be firm in certain opinions but civil in their expression. Sometimes, of course, the logic and reason break down,[5] but on the whole the *Freeholder* is vintage Addison. It is remarkable for the interplay of imagination and party purpose.

The variety of tone in the first ten *Freeholders* is typical of the way Addison modulates the tenor and varies the technique of all fifty-five numbers. Number 1 is a straightforward statement of the Freeholder's pride in his rights as an Englishman which all his fellow-citizens "enjoy in common with myself" and which are "secured by his majesty's title, his administration, and his personal character." Number 2 is a flattering portrait of his majesty George I. Number 3 is a humorous, fictitious memoir written by a rebel officer; it describes a Quixote-like campaign in which Jacobite soldiers attack cows and sheep instead of enemy troops, drink taverns dry, and win the hearts of pretty harlots. Number 4 is a "fair-sex" and tongue-in-cheek paper which hopes that, if beautiful ladies realize how their freedoms and entertainments depend on Protestant liberty, "it lies in the power of every fine woman, to secure at least half a dozen able-bodied men to his Majesty's service" for "arguments out of a pretty mouth are unanswerable."

Number 5 returns to a sober tone to analyze the virtue of patriotism. Number 6, on the sacredness of oaths taken to uphold the king, is likewise serious. Number 7, in the spirit of the *Whig-Examiner,* attacks directly the character and principles of the Pretender's supporters. Number 8 is another paper directed at the ladies, showing that virgins ought to help the government by rebuffing rebel suitors, that wives should nag husbands into loyalty, and that all women can unite into a "Female Association" pledged to the use of beauty and wiles for the preservation of the king. Number 9 is a point-by-point refutation of the Pretender's claims that George does not love his subjects, lacks the support of the Church and Parliament, and keeps a rightful heir from the throne. Number 10 avers that "the gross of the people . . . are whigs in their hearts" who prefer the prosperity of constitutional rule to the depression of despotism; the story of Morocco's Muley Ishmael, a good man who turned into a tyrannical ruler when given absolute power, illustrates the fatal results that would flow from the Pretender's victory.

Especially interesting to note in these first ten papers is the placement of humorous ones. They anticipate the serious discussion of the issues. The mindless campaigning of the rebels and the coquettish loyalty of women precede the dissertations on patriotism and oath-taking. The ladies' handling of rebel lovers or husbands sympathetic to the Pretender prefigures the *Freeholder's* response to the Pretender's claims. This order of discussion seems to make the Sunday-schoolishness of the moralistic essays more tolerable. After stupidity and lightheadedness, a sermon might sound intelligent and calm. Addison's technique here, reminiscent of the balance in the *Spectator,* where ideals are presented straightforwardly and deviations into nonsense humorously, characterizes the sequence of *Freeholders.* Some papers are spontaneous responses to developments during the rebellion, but on the whole the *Freeholder* series is a carefully orchestrated periodical.

The technique can be seen at work in Addison's best comic papers, those on the Tory fox-hunters, with which Samuel Johnson claimed "Bigotry itself must be delighted."[6] Numbers 22,

44, and 47 made explicit what had been implicit in the portrait of Sir Roger de Coverley: that the predominantly Tory class of country squires were not men to whom the government of England ought to be trusted. The first Fox-hunter precedes the discussion of the impracticability of rebellion and of the need for stability in government (*Freeholders* 24 and 25); the last two by contrast introduce the faithful creator of political stability, the experienced minister (*Freeholder* 48), and public celebration of the Protestant succession as the ideal of political community: "nothing is more beautiful in the sight of God and man, than a king and his people concurring in such extraordinary acts of devotion" (*Freeholder* 49).

Freeholder 22 leisurely introduces the Tory Fox-hunter whom the Freeholder meets as he rides in a rural county and lets him reveal in conversation his own foibles and prejudices. The Fox-hunter romanticizes the Stuart past (he thinks there has been no good weather since the Revolution), insults out of hand any man he suspects of Whig principles (like the Examiner, he calls them all whelps and curs), despises foreign trade (although he drinks a punch composed of imported ingredients), and is generally a conceited, dull, and superstitious fellow. The day's acquaintance ends with the Freeholder, the Fox-Hunter, and another local squire at a tavern:

We sat pretty late over our punch; and, midst a great deal of improving discourse, drank the healths of several persons in the country, whom I had never heard of, that, they both assured me, were the ablest statesmen in the nation; and of some Londoners, whom they extolled to the skies for their wit and who, I knew, passed in town for silly fellows.

It being now midnight, and my friend perceiving by his almanack that the moon was up, he called for his horses, and took a sudden resolution to go to his house, which was at three miles' distance from the town, after having bethought himself that he never slept well out of his own bed. He shook me very heartily by the hand at parting, and discovered a great air of satisfaction in his looks, that he had met with an opportunity of showing his parts, and left me a much wiser man than he found me. (*Freeholder* 22)

This character of an essentially ignorant and gullible squire is handled a little less roughly later on although Addison's point that he is not to be entrusted with government is unchanged. In the former paper the Fox-hunter witnesses a mummers' parade and has great difficulty distinguishing the real people from the characters whom they impersonate. In the latter the Fox-hunter is reconciled to King George when a London tour demonstrates that all the Pretender's propaganda proves false. England is not in ruins. Churches are going up, not coming down; the rumored omens of sick lions at the zoo and a toppled statue of King Charles are mere invention; life and business run normally in the streets of London; and even the family of Hanovers is not monstrous after all. When the Fox-hunter sees the king's children, their innocence, beauty, and sweetness complete his conversion.

Because of the political issues at stake, some of the humor is rather obvious and the terms of the Fox-hunter's conversion predictable. But in his best manner, Addison's comedy is economical and tempered. The nature of the medium and the circumstances of the occasion dictated that all the *Freeholder* essays would be fairly obvious and predictable. Addison's achievement here, as it was in "The Campaign," was to make entertaining and readable what was expected. The *Freeholder* has never ranked with the letters of Junius or Burke's *Reflections on the Revolution in France* as great political literature; it seems more like a position paper by which a ministry reassures the citizenry. For this undertaking, Addison was rewarded with the post of a Commissioner of Trade and Plantation.

Chapter Eight
Drama

Addison's three plays are a disparate group: an opera, *Rosamond* (1707); a tragedy, *Cato* (1713); and a comedy, *The Drummer* (1716). They reflect the directions that theater was to move in through the eighteenth century: the combination of music and drama, political drama dressed in classical garb, and sentimental comedy which replaced laughter with the sympathetic presentation of virtue in distress.

Neither *Rosamond* nor *The Drummer* had much success on stage; each ran for only three performances at first production. *Rosamond,* seeking to capitalize on the taste of London theater-goers for Italian style opera (in which all words are sung), failed because of Thomas Clayton's atrocious musical score. *The Drummer* was a little ahead of the vogue for sentimental comedy; its combination of morality and humor was still a little too delicate for most audiences.[1] Both plays were revived with better success later in the century. *Rosamond* was set to a new musical score, and *The Drummer* reappeared when sentiment was in flower.

Cato, Addison's only tragedy, had great success on the stage; it ran for over thirty performances. The success was due, however, less to its dramatic virtues than to the occasion. Addison had worked on the play years before but received friendly criticism from Arthur Maynwaring and Colley Cibber that it was unsuitable for production. In 1713, through, anything that treated politics, as *Cato* did, was cannon-fodder for the literary warfare between Whig and Tory. John Hughes who had assisted with the *Spectator,* persuaded Addison to finish the play and allow its production to revive the "old British {read Whig} spirit of liberty."[2] As a matter of fact, *Cato* offers such general political sentiments that both parties could and did applaud it mightily.

None of Addison's plays is a great one, but none is bad. Admittedly all three suffer from distinct and serious flaws, as well as one common failing, the lack of believable or interesting central characters. In general, however, they deserve more credit than literary histories usually begrudge. *Rosamond* and *The Drummer* contain some of Addison's best comic characters and sprightly dialogue. *Cato*'s blank verse is probably the best poetry Addison wrote.

Rosamond

Addison's *Rosamond* was meant to be entirely sung. No wonder Clayton's abominable score meant the failure of the opera. Not content with one explanation, however, subsequent critics have attempted to specify other reasons for *Rosamond's* failure. One suggests that little action happens,[3] another that the humor is "flat and forced,"[4] and a third that the short lines required by the singing are displeasing, especially the meter in which the leading comic character Sir Trusty speaks: "by the introduction of which he [Addison] has so strangely debased and degraded his elegant opera."[5]

The play's initial failure and subsequent lack of reputation are a surprise considering the ingredients which Addison mixed into his operatic recipe. Its story of Henry II's love for Rosamond Clifford was taken from English history and was the stuff of popular legend. The characters were standard: the royal couple torn by the love-and-honor conflict typical of heroic drama, paralleled by a comic couple whose mismatched love was the staple of Restoration comedy. The setting of the play was contemporary, Woodstock Park, where Queen Anne was currently building Blenheim Palace as a monument to the famous campaign of 1704. The third act indeed has a spectacular effect of the medieval king granted a vision of the future palace. The theme is equally modern, the assertion of Christian virtues and marital fidelity as hallmarks of a reformed code of manners for ladies and gentlemen.

A brief relation of the plot will show how Addison merged character, setting, and theme. In Act I, as Queen Elinor and her page walk in Woodstock Park, they come to the bower where

Henry II's mistress, Rosamond, lives. Proximity to her husband's lover enrages the queen, who determines to win back her Henry's affection. The bower is guarded by Sir Trusty, a physically aging but emotionally youthful courtier, who also is in love with Rosamond. But because of his jealous wife, Grideline, and a royal rival like Henry, Sir Trusty cannot make public his love. Rosamond is as unhappy as the queen or Sir Trusty; she worries when Henry is away fighting in France, and she feels guilty for their illicit relationship. When Henry returns from war, he rushes to the bower, thinking only of his sweet mistress.

Act II begins with the love-talk of Henry and Rosamond, which lasts until state business calls him away for a few hours. Meanwhile, Grideline, suspicious because Sir Trusty is foppishly attentive to his dress and manners, assumes her husband has become Rosmond's lover and sends her page to spy on the bower. The page does not find the supposed lovers; instead he finds Queen Elinor in a jealous passion contemplating murder. The queen hesitates to kill Rosamond only because she fears the girl's death may lead to Henry's own, or to his final rejection of his queen. Overcoming her irresolution, the queen confronts Rosamond with a choice: she may commit suicide or be stabbed. Rosamond chooses suicide by drinking poison and falls to the ground. Likewise, when Sir Trusty finds the corpse, frustrated passion and fear of Henry's anger drive him to drink from the fatal cup.

Act III discovers Henry asleep in the grotto. Two angels, "the Guardian spirits of the British Kings in War and Peace," visit him and fill his mind with dreams of martial conquest and royal fame to ease his love-sickness. They assure Henry a view of the future, of the hero Marlborough in the reign of Queen Anne. Henry awakens, determined to give up Rosamond's love. On learning of her death, the king decides to die heroically in battle. To avoid this fatal resolve, the queen reveals her secret: the poison has only cast Rosamond and Sir Trusty into a deathlike sleep for a day. Rosamond has been taken to a convent to expiate her sin. Relieved, Henry promises to live as faithful husband to Elinor. The queen in turn forgives his faithlessness. Each looks upon the other with renewed love. Trusty awakens to find marital harmony the new law of the land and determines to live and love with only Grideline.

One critic has commented that *Rosamond* was ahead of its time; it was not an opera but a modern musical comedy.[6] From the summary of the plot one sees that Sir Trusty has a great deal of stage time; from reading the play one realizes that Trusty also has the best lines. As in Broadway musicals like *Guys and Dolls* or *Oklahoma!*, the liveliest and most interesting characters are the comic and level-of-life second leads, not the romantic and idealized first leads. In *Rosamond* Sir Trusty has the best part.

Mixed serious and comic plots were a staple of Italian opera as well as of the theater, but until the operettas of Gilbert and Sullivan the aristocrats in the serious plot generally kept their dignity amid the play of their underlings. *Rosamond* is closer to the Gilbert and Sullivan mode, however, than to its contemporaries. Trusty is involved with all the serious characters, Henry, Rosamond and the queen, and usually manages to make them appear lame stereotypes or to undercut their dignified passions with his buffoonery. Two examples should make the point that while little may happen in terms of dramatic action in *Rosamond*, a great deal happens in the juxtaposition of high and low characters.

When King Henry enters for the first time in the play, he is filled with passionate longing to see his beloved Rosamond. Sir Trusty, however, is just as anxious to win his lord's favor by a proper and dignified greeting. Their conversation at cross-purposes is the stuff of great comedy:

> *K. Hen.* Where is my love! my *Rosamond*!
> *Trust.* First, as in strictest duty bound,
> I kiss your royal hand,
> *K. Hen.* Where is my life! my *Rosamond*!
> *Trust.* Next with submission most profound,
> I welcome you to land.
> *K. Hen.* Where is the tender, charming fair!

Trust.	Let me appear, great Sir, I pray,
	Methodical in what I say.
K. Hen.	Where is my love, O tell me where!
Trust.	For when we have a Prince's ear,
	We should have wit,
	To know what's fit
	For us to speak, and him to hear.
K. Hen.	These dull delays I cannot bear.
	Where is my love, O tell me where! (I. vi 1–16)

Similarly, at the end of Act II, when the queen has apparently murdered Rosamond by forcing her to drink poison, Trusty discovers her corpse and takes his own life both out of his love for Rosamond and his fear of the king. In between Rosamond's conventional vow to haunt her murderess and the queen's conventional rejoicing in the dispatch of a rival comes Trusty's suicide soliloquy. It is the hammed-up, exaggerated demise that every second-rate actor has ever imagined a death speech should be. Significantly, Trusty's death speech is as long as Rosamond's and longer than the queen's triumph:

> [*Sir* Trusty *in a Fright.*]
> A breathless corps! what have I seen!
> And follow'd by the jealous Queen!
> It must be she! my fears are true:
> The bowl of pois'nous juice I view.
> How can the fam'd Sir *Trusty* live
> To hear his Master chide and grieve?
> No! tho' I hate such bitter beer,
> Fair *Rosamond,* I'll pledge thee here. [*Drinks.*]
>   The King this doleful news shall read
>   In lines of my inditing:
> "*Great Sir,*   [*Writes.*]
>   "Your *Rosamond* is dead
>   "As I am at this present writing.
> *The bower turns round, my brain's abus'd,*
> *The Labyrinth grows more confus'd,*
> *The thickets dance—I stretch, I yawn.*

> *Death has tripp'd up my heels—I'm gone.*
> > [Staggers and falls.]
> > > (II. vii. 1–17)

Thus a great deal of comedy comes not from action but from the juxtaposition of incongruous attitudes toward love and death. The comic scenes of *Rosamond* benefit as well from the short poetic lines said to be so "unpleasing" for the development of the serious passions in the play. Early in the play Trusty tries to soothe the suspicions of his wife that he loves another woman; once he has done so he immediately proceeds to arouse them once again. The short-lines verse is perfect for expressing the shallow and transitory emotional lives of the speakers:

> *Grid.* Faithless varlet, art thou there?
> *Trust.* My love, my dove, my charming fair!
> *Grid.* Monster, thy wheedling tricks I know.
> *Trust.* Why wilt thou call thy turtle so?
> *Grid.* Cheat not me with false caresses.
> *Trust.* Let me stop thy mouth with kisses.
> *Grid.* Those to fair *Rosamond* are due.
> *Trust.* She is not half so fair as you.
> *Grid.* She views thee with a lover's eye.
> *Trust.* I'll still be thine, and let her die.
> *Grid.* No, no, 'tis plain. Thy frauds I see,
> > Traitor to thy King and me!
> Trust. O Grideline! *consult thy glass,*
> > *Behold that sweet bewitching face,*
> > *Those blooming cheeks, that lovely hue!*
> > > *Ev'ry feature*
> > > > *(Charming creature)*
> > *Will convince you I am true.*
> Grid. *O how blest were* Grideline,
> > *Could I call Sir* Trusty *mine!*
> > *Did he not cover amorous wiles*
> > *With soft, but ah! deceiving smiles:*
> > *How should I revel in delight,*
> > *The spouse of such a peerless Knight!*
> *Trust.* At length the storm begins to cease,
> > I've sooth'd and flatter'd her to peace.

	'Tis now my turn to tyrannize: [*Aside.*]
	I feel, I feel my fury rise!
	Tigress, be gone.
Grid.	_____ I love thee so.
	I cannot go.
Trust.	Fly from my passion, Beldame, fly!
Grid.	Why so unkind, Sir *Trusty*, why?
Trust.	Thou'rt the plague of my life.
Grid.	I'm a foolish, fond wife.
Trust.	Let us part,
	Let us part.
Grid.	Will you break my poor heart?
	Will you break my poor heart?
Trust.	I will if I can.
Grid.	O barbarous man!
	From whence doth all this passion flow?
Trust.	*Thou art ugly and old,*
	And a villainous scold.
Grid.	*Thou art a rustick to call me so.*
	I'm not ugly nor old,
	Nor a villainous scold,
	But thou art a rustick to call me so.
	Thou, Traitor, adieu!
Trust.	*Farewel, thou Shrew!*
Grid.	*Thou Traitor,*
Trust.	*Thou Shrew,*
Both.	*Adieu! adieu!* (I. iii. 1–54)

Of course Addison was not deliberately inventing a new genre; he was merely mixing the conventions of the age. The domination of the comic element in Rosamond is evidence rather of Addison's true talents. Whether in his poetry, where his Latin mock heroics please more than many of his serious English poems, or in his prose where the comic or satiric *Spectators* outshine the moralizing papers, Addison's most readable quality is his humor. As Samuel Johnson concluded his favorable analysis of the play, "If Addison had cultivated the lighter parts of poetry, he would probably have excelled."[7]

Cato

Addison's tragedy about Marcus Portius Cato the Younger, the Roman republican who died fighting the dictatorship of Julius Caesar, earned the popular success which *Rosamond* did not. After its first performance in April 1713, it ran for thirty nights, an unprecedented performance for the time. One contemporary caught the popular opinion when he hailed *Cato* as the first "perfect piece" upon the English stage in many years.[8] The play was rapidly translated into or imitated in French, Italian, and Latin. *Cato* soon secured an international reputation. Voltaire congratulated Addison for writing the first "rational tragedy" in English.[9] Later in the century *Cato* was performed before George Washington's troops at Valley Forge (1777) as inspiration to fight on against tyranny.[10] In the early nineteenth century Cato was the favorite role of the tragedian John Kemble, who thought the play " the utmost sublimity of tragedy."[11]

But *Cato*'s reputation has not lasted. Most modern critics think the play has too much declamation, moralizing, and silly love intriguing. Many find the hero an unattractive tragic figure: one finds him "an intolerable prig"[12] and another thinks he has too little to do.[13] Most historians of drama regard *Cato* as a museum piece and shudder at the thought that anyone would ever put it on the stage.

The reasoning behind the modern reaction becomes clear from a recitation of the plot. The main plot is interesting but hardly tragic. Cato and his army have been trapped at Utica by the superior forces of Julius Caesar. Cato is the last hope of the Roman Republic; he has led the forces of the senate in futile resistance to Caesar's attempt to become dictator. At Utica Cato faces all the unhappy predicaments of a cornered commander. His troops teeter on the edge of mutiny; his allies threaten to decamp. He does not know whether to offer final hopeless battle, or to surrender, content that fighting as long as possible is heroism enough, or to depart in a forlorn search for new allies, or to commit suicide and achieve final independence from Caesar. Amid awesome problems and dreadful choices Cato struggles against panic to remain in control of himself and of events. Cato's plight is none of his fault; superior forces and the will of the gods have overwhelmed him. In a final gesture to remain master of his own destiny, he commits suicide.

The subplot, on the other hand, which provides most of the motivation and most of the action, sounds soap-opera silly. Cato's two sons, Marcus and Portius, love the same girl, Lucia. Marcus does not know his rival is his brother; Portius knows and feels guilty; Lucia knows which brother she prefers but is reluctant to say for fear of hurting either. Cato's daughter, Marcia, is likewise loved by two. Sempronius, a Roman senator, loves her enough to turn traitor if Caesar will allow Marcia to be his reward. Juba, a Numidian prince, loves Marcia, too, but Cato himself discourages the prince from courtship while the army is trapped. Although she loves Juba, Marcia refuses to listen to his wooing until their political fate is decided. Desperate for Marcia, Sempronius plans a mutiny of Roman troops to overthrow Cato and carry off the girl. He gains the help of Syphax, Juba's advisor, who wants to lead the allied forces out of dangerous Utica and back to the safety of Numidia. The rebellion brings the lovers' predicaments out into the open. When Sempronius, disguised as Juba, is killed, Marcia cries over the corpse, leading Juba to think she loved his rival. Meanwhile, Marcus sends Portius on the uncomfortable mission of wooing Lucia for him; when Portius cannot report that Lucia favors his suit, Marcus despairingly throws himself into battle against the Numidian rebels. His death fortunately solves the dilemma of Lucia and Portius, leaving them free to acknowledge their mutual love; and the misunderstanding between Juba and Marcia is quickly resolved. Cato's burden is lightened somewhat by the heroic death of one son and the proper marriages of his other children.

But *Cato* is one of those works to which summary does not do justice; summary here simply highlights weaknesses. Addison's drama is not theater or tragedy as we ordinarily think of them. *Cato* ought to be discussed with Addison's poetry for it is essentially a closet drama. An accident of history, the political fervor of 1713, brought to the stage a play which Addison himself had probably come to think was inappropriate for production. Everything about the play—its theme, its literary tradition, its conformity with Addison's views on tragedy, its elevated and formal use of image patterns, and its self-conscious use of discursive, mirroring subplots—points to *Cato* as a work better read than acted. The judgment of an eighteenth-century reviewer recognized the distinction which must not be forgotten:

. . . we must absolutely deny its theatrical excellence; it is certainly a moral, colloquial poem of great merit, but a tragedy full of defects; it should be immortal in the closet, but cannot justly claim possession of the stage. [14]

Why did Addison choose Cato as his subject? In his Oxford years he found Roman writers almost unanimous in their admiration of Cato, who committed suicide in 46 B.C. after a decade of fighting Caesar. Plutarch's "Life of Cato" pictures him as the active and faithful magistrate, in turn quaestor, consul, and senator. In Lucan's epic poem *The Civil War*, Cato is a fearless and tough general who shares the hardships of his soldiers. In Cicero's *On the Ends of Good and Evil*, Cato is the spokesman for the stern virtue of Stoic philosophy. Seneca sums up the portrait of Cato among ancient writers in a description which almost deifies the man and which Addison chose as the epigraph to the play:

Behold a sight worthy of God himself, intent upon his own works, to witness. Here is God's equal in worth, a brave man calm amid misfortunes. I see not, I say, that Jupiter has on earth anything more beautiful, if he wished to inspire the soul, than the sight of Cato, his allies already beaten time and again, nonetheless erect amid the ruins of the state.

In Cato Addison found that model of Roman citizenship, the intelligent and cultivated service to the state, which became the standard of his own career. When Juba commends the virtues of a Roman soul, he is expressing Addison's essential view of Cato:

A *Roman* soul is bent on higher views:
To civilize the rude unpolish'd world,

And lay it under the restraint of laws;
To make Man mild, and sociable to Man;
To cultivate the wild licentious Savage
With wisdom, discipline, and liberal arts;
Th' embellishments of life: Virtues like these,
Make human nature shine, reform the soul,
And break our fierce barbarians into men. (I. iv.

But Cato was a figure of more than personal preference; he was a figure significant to the age. One of Mary Wortley Montagu's comments on the draft of *Cato* makes clear how widely known and how powerful a figure for Augustan England was the Stoic senator. "The Figure that Great Man makes in History," she writes, "is so noble and at the same time so Simple, I hardly beleivd [*sic*] it possible to shew him on our stage. He appears here in all his Beauty; his sentiments are great, and express'd without affectation; his Language is Sublime without Fustian, and smooth without a misbecoming softnesse. I hear a Roman with all the Plain Greatness of Ancient Rome."[15] Cato's "plain greatness" reached almost mythic proportions among Addison's contemporaries.[16] Augustan England looked to Rome for models of personal character and public conduct: for pagan and secular virtues to replace the Christian ideals that had created fanaticism and rebellion in the Civil War, and for principles of political stability that were constitutional instead of theocratic. The story of Cato was varied and adaptable to these purposes.

The academic heritage of *Cato* is evident in Addison's choice of form as well as of theme. The dramatic model for the play is Senecan tragedy which emphasizes in dialogue the discussion of ideas and downplays theatricality. Addison sets *Cato* in the critical time of Rome's transition from republic to dictatorship; the revolution tests the patriotism and ambition of each character. As a result the internal struggle of the characters resembles the outward turmoil of the state. The condition of the soul, however, is Addison's concern. No wonder, apart from any natural diffidence, he was reluctant to see *Cato* produced. Its political sentiments (love of country, praise of freedom, antipathy to civil war) are so general that men of any party could profess them.

Addison's attention focuses on the personal drama that accompanies political upheaval: necessity for fortitude, confidence in Providence, personal abnegation. *Cato,* revised and completed in 1713, reflects also Addison's discussion of tragedy in *Spectators* 39, 40, 42, 44.[17] The premise ; Senecan, "a virtuous man . . . struggling with misfoi. .ine." Cato is blameless for the failure of his cause or the problems that overtake his associates and family; he rather endures the woes that the mysterious ways of the gods impose. (A perceptive reviewer noted the dramatic cost: "This Tragedy has not that wonderful *Pereptie* or Change of Fortune and Discovery, which we find in the *Oedipus* of *Sophocles.*"[18]) Through the depiction of virtuous endurance tragedies "cherish and cultivate that humanity which is the ornament of our nature. They soften insolence, soothe reflection, and subdue the mind to the dispositions of Providence." Tragedies best achieve these effects by the use of language rather than by spectacular stage production or elaborate costume. An audience is moved by "noble sentiment that is depressed with homely language," free of "sounding phrases, hard metaphors, and forced expression." *Cato* invites its audience to observe a portrait of human greatness instead of a sequence of human actions.

But if the parts of the play which were enjoyed most were "where *Cato* suspends the Action and Passion of the Scene to teach the Audience, Philosophy and Morality,"[19] these precepts do not come naked and unadorned. Addison dresses them, as he has always dressed lessons in private or public mores, in the garb of description, simile and metaphor. Addison's language has always attracted and continues to attract attention. Most recently the imagery of the play—a pattern clustering about images of storm, wind and water—has received attention, both as a device typical of Whig writers for expressing a political stand and as a way of universalizing the political and romantic tensions of the play.[20] More to Addison's purpose, perhaps, is that the imagery of storm is a traditional way of illustrating the virtue of the Stoic philosopher in general and of Cato in particular. Cicero, historically Cato's sometime ally and sometime foe in the disputes of

the Roman Senate, attacked those who would tarnish that famous
name of Cato:

> ignorant as they were what strength there is in character, in integrity,
> in greatness of soul, and in that virtue which remains unshaken by
> violent storms; which shines in darkness; which though dislodged still
> abides and remains unmoved from its true home; is radiant always by
> its own light and is never sullied by the baseness of others.[21]

This is the central image of the play: the stern Cato, calm
amid the tumult of civil war, whose virtue glows as a beacon to
other men. In the play, admirers and enemies alike acknowledge
the steadfastness of the man. Cato's son Portius acclaims:

> How does the lustre of our father's actions,
> Through the dark cloud of Ills that cover him,
> Break out, and burn with more triumphant brightness!
> His sufferings shine, and spread a glory round him. (I. i. 27–30)

Sempronius, dedicated as he is to Cato's downfall, must exclaim:

> Thou hast seen mount *Atlas*:
> While storms and tempests thunder on its brows,
> And oceans break their billows at its feet,
> It stands ummoved, and glories in its height.
> Such is that haughty man. . . . (II. vi. 11–14)

But just as Cato is the standard of human virtue in the play
toward which the other characters aspire or against which they
conspire, so too the imagery of the storm and light reveals how
characters and their actions come close or turn away from the
norm of Cato. Those who are like Cato stand serenely amid the
storm while their virtue glows calmly and steadily in the wind.
Those who are unlike Cato discover that the storm is within as
well as without; their souls flame rather than glow—and just as
flame blazes one moment and dies the next, their souls unsteadily
react to the temptations and duties of life. Addison makes imagery
the index of character and the chronometer of plot. Each character's virtue will be tested by an emotion of some sort—self-

interest, lust, love, jealousy, fear. In figurative terms, each character's interior calm will be shattered by a hurricane or a whirlwind. Those who are not Cato-like will be destroyed; those
striving to become Cato-like will be hardened; those already Cato-
like will endure. And Cato himself will triumph by controlling
his own fate.

Sempronius' "furious soul," as Juba calls it, stands in contrast
to Cato's. Instead of standing firm amid the storms and chaos
of the world, it is caught up in the tempest. As Cato warns
Sempronius at one point, "Let not the torrent of impetuous zeal /
Transport thee thus beyond the bounds of reason." Sempronius,
however, delights in the disorder of storms, whether in politics
or in love. The image he uses to the mutineers to describe their
effect on Cato reveals Sempronius' delight in passion and revenge:

> At length the winds are rais'd, the storm blows high,
> Be it your care, my friends, to keep it up
> In its full fury, and direct it right,
> 'Till it has spent itself on *Cato's* head. (III. iv. 1–4)

Likewise his love for Marcia seeks not her calm virtue but the
transporting passion of rape:

> How will my bosom swell with anxious joy,
> When I behold her struggling in my arms,
> With glowing beauty, and disorder'd charms,
> While fear and anger, with alternate grace,
> Pant in her breast, and vary in her face! (III. vii. 26–30)

Sempronious, as rebel and conqueror, is the image of Caesar,
whose "active soul" conquers Nature and delights in havoc:

> . . . in vain has Nature form'd
> Mountains and oceans to oppose his passage;
> He bounds o'er all, victorious in his march;
> The *Alpes* and *Pyreneans* sink before him,
> Through winds and waves and storms he works his way,
> Impatient for the battle. . . . (I. iii. 11–17)

Sempronius, however, finds himself incapable of controlling the
storm of rebellion he unleashes and dies in the very whirlwind
which he and his co-conspirator Syphax thought would over-
whelm Cato:

> I laugh to think how your unshaken *Cato*
> Will look aghast, while unforeseen destruction
> Pours in upon him thus from every side.
> So, where our wide *Numidian* wastes extend,
> Sudden, th' impetuous hurricanes descend,
> Wheel through the air, in circling eddies play,
> Tear up the sands, and sweep whole plains away.
> The helpless traveller, with wild surprize,
> Sees the dry desart all around him rise,
> And smother'd in the dusty whirlwind dies. (II. vi. 48–57)

Marcus, Cato's son, is like Sempronius, one whose soul is as
restless as the storm without. His love for Lucia meets the same
frustrations as Sempronius' love for Marcia. Likewise his love is
beyond his ability to control. Marcia warns the beloved Lucia
about her brother's passion:

> Whene'er he speaks of thee, his heart's in flames,
> He sends out all his soul in every word,
> And thinks, and talks, and looks like one transported.
> Unhappy youth! how will thy coldness raise
> Tempests and storms in his afflicted bosom! (I. vi. 55–59)

But Marcus is more virtuous than Sempronius in this way: if
Lucia cannot be convinced by persuasion, he will not carry her
off by force. Marcus can direct his passion into Rome's cause.
When Syphax's rebellion breaks out, after Portius' interview with
Lucia has failed to win her for Marcus, the rejected brother glories
in the death that battle offers. Reckless love drives Marcus, like
Sempronius, into fatal combat; unlike Sempronius, Marcus dies
a Roman warrior hero at Utica's gates rather than a disguised
Numidian in the women's tents. Marcus recognizes the virtues
of his father and Rome's cause although he cannot stifle his passion
for Lucia. Marcus lives out Portius' prophecy:

I know thy gen'rous temper well;
Fling but th' appearance of dishonour on it,
It strait takes fire, and mounts into a blaze. (I. i. 96–98)

Though uncontrollable, the blaze is at least a signal fire of Roman virtue.

Juba, born a Numidian but growing into a Cato-like Roman, is tempted from the political crisis at hand by his love, as are Sempronius and Marcus. But his love for Marcia is more controlled and more easily subdued to the political demands of the situation. His teachers are at hand: Cato lectures him on virtue, and Marcia quickly parries his love talk to send him back to the battlefield. Juba is a naturally good man whose virtue is strengthened by philosophy and Cato. When Syphax tries to argue that every Numidian hunter who goes without sleep and accepts desert hardships is the equal of the Roman Stoic, Juba rebuts the claim: "Thy prejudice, *Syphax,* won't discern / What virtues grow from ignorance and choice." Juba's commitment is tested by Cato's refusal to hear his plea for Marcia's hand in marriage as long as the war rages. Syphax attempts to seduce the disappointed suitor by invoking the elemental forces of passion:

Juba commands *Numidia*'s hardy troops,
Mounted on steeds, unused to the restraint
Of curbes or bittes, and fleeter than the winds:
Give but the word, we'll snatch this damsel up,
And bear her off. (II. v. 30–34)

But Juba's control withstands the temptation, as it does his momentary misinterpretation of Marcia's outburst over Sempronius' corpse clad in his garments. For standing firm on the side of virtue, Juba wins Marcia's love and Cato's praise.

Marcia, Lucia and Portius are all alike. As the play opens they are the characters most firmly fixed in Cato's model. Each has eyes mainly on the father's plight despite distracting cares; Marcia, her love for Juba; Lucia, a terrible choice between brothers who love her; Portius, at once friend and rival to Marcus. All

three are unlike the previous characters; not their own weaknesses
will ever distract their attention from the holy light of Cato's
example. Rather the reckless passions of Sempronius and Marcus
will buffet them and force out into the open the emotions which
each, successfully but not without difficulty, hides and controls.
Only the accident of believing Juba dead releases the "tumultuous
tides" of Marcia's love for him, and distracts her from Cato's
plight. Only Marcus' forcing Portius to speak his love to Lucia
causes these lovers hardship. To avoid choosing one brother over
the other, Lucia postpones a decision "while such a cloud of
mischiefs hangs about us." And her decisive non-decision is Portius' dark cloud; ". . . here / Such an unlook'd for storm of ills
falls on me, / It beats down all my strength." Yet Marcia, Lucia
and Portius are all ultimately strong, like Cato, amid the blasts
of unreason, fear or jealousy. None are lost to a frustrated passion;
all purge themselves by will and self-discipline, as the striking
image which closes Act I predicts:

> So the pure limpid stream when foul with stains,
> Of rushing torrents, and descending rains,
> Works it self clear, and as it runs, refines;
> 'Till by degrees, the floating mirrour shines,
> Reflects each flow'r that on the border grows,
> And a new Heaven in its fair bosom shows. (I. vi. 82–87)

Cato, himself, is always the "floating mirrour." The action of
the play dramatizes the image which Cicero gave, of the brave
man calm amid the storms of ruin. In Act II, Cato urges a wait-
and-see policy to the Senate, which is torn between the surrender
advocated by Lucius and the all-out assault urged by Sempronius.
In the same act, Caesar's envoy Decius warns Cato, "Think on
the storm that gathers o'er your head, / And threatens every hour
to burst upon it." To which Cato responds with a brave speech
that indicts Caesar for crimes against Rome and reaffirms his own
willingness to die rather than surrender to a tyrant. Cato resolves
to endure any tempest, and the rest of the play proves his resolve.
   In Act III Cato stands firm amid the fury of the rebellion by
Sempronius' troops. Rather than run from the storm, Cato seeks

out the rebels and confronts them. His speech to them, like the speech to Decius, stresses the endurance of personal hardship for the greater cause of Rome. Cato reminds the troops of the hardships they shared in the Libyan desert. If this memory does not move them, Cato would willingly see them go off to Caesar to complain: "You could not undergo the toils of war, / Nor bear the hardships that your leader bore." The rebels lose their passion in tears, and Cato has withstood another shock.

In Act IV the storm which breaks upon Cato is personal and more intense. Syphax leads the Numidian cavalry in flight from Utica. This second rebellion is difficult even for the Stoic to accept: "*Lucius,* the torrent bears too hard upon me," Cato confides. Then Cato learns that Marcus has died trying to halt the break-out. Cato ought to sink under this second blow, but he is instead buoyed. In doing his duty, killing Syphax and stopping the rebels, Marcus has done as Cato did previously and thus recalls to his father his own strict standard. Cato comforts those who would shed tears over Marcus by reminding them that personal loss matters little at the moment when " 'Tis *Rome* requires our tears."

With Caesar drawing near and the remnants of his forces about to escape, Cato contemplates his own death.[22] Here is the greatest threat to the "brave man calm amid misfortunes." He feels ". . . this secret dread, and inward horror, / Of falling into nought," the prospect which "shadows, clouds, and darkness rest upon. . . ." But even the awesomeness of death and unknown eternity cannot discompose Cato. Plato's book on the immortality of the soul reassures him that the soul will rest in its virtue not only amid the storms of earthly life but amid any storm, even the dissolution of the world. Cato says,

But this informs me I shall never die.
The soul, secured in her existence, smiles
At the drawn dagger, and defies its point.
The stars shall fade away, the sun himself
Grow dim with age, and Nature sink in years,
But thou shalt flourish in immortal youth,

Unhurt amidst the war of elements,
The wrecks of matter, and the crush of worlds. (V. i. 24–31)

His own death, far from holding any more than momentary fear
for Cato, is in fact his moment of triumph, his greatest assertion
of his own steadiness amid the wreck of the world. Whatever
fleets or armies Caesar may have, Cato "shall open to himself a
passage, / And mock thy hopes."

Cato, like all the characters, then, is motivated and acts within
the framework of an imagery that contrasts interior calm with
interior disorder and pictures the ideal of interior order amid
exterior destruction. The struggle is not without a plan, although
the gods seem to have abandoned the virtuous man and heaped
reward on the vicious one. Cato explains the purpose to Juba,
once more employing the basic imagery:

The Gods, in bounty, work up storms about us,
That give mankind occasion to exert
Their hidden strength, and throw out into practice
Virtues, which shun the day, and lie conceal'd
In the smooth seasons and the calms of life. (II. iv. 54–58)

While Cato speaks for a consistency in virtue that is admirable,
he seems to lack adequate human motivation. In Act IV his
behavior on viewing Marcus' corpse, for instance, is rigid enough
to be monstrous instead of admirable. Likewise his advice to
Portius, to retire to the family estate and accept the dictum of
fate, hardly squares with his own reaction to Caesar's conquest
or with his recent praise of Marcus' death. Cato also lacks any
sign of doubt or fear about the eternal questions he poses. His
one moment of weakness, as he lies dying and wonders if he may
have fallen on his sword too soon, occurs quickly and is passed
over with a shrug. Addison imbues Cato with the ideals that
impress an audience but not with the humanity that captures the
imagination.

As is often the case with Addison, Samuel Johnson deserves
the last word. As critical of Addison as Johnson often is no man
has been more astute in seeing exactly what credit Addison de-

serves. Johnson explains that *Cato* has the mark of poetry—the best words in the best order—but not the mark of drama—the imaginative engagement of human passion. In comparing Addison and Shakespeare, Johnson writes,

. . . *Addison* speaks the language of poets, and *Shakespeare,* of men. We find in *Cato* innumerable beauties which enamour us of its authour, but we see nothing that acquaints us with human sentiments or human actions; we place it with the fairest and the noblest progeny which judgment propagates by conjunction with learning, but *Othello* is the vigorous and vivacious offspring of observation impregnated by genius. *Cato* affords a splendid exhibition of artificial and fictitious manners, and delivers just and noble sentiments, in diction easy, elevated and harmonious, but its hopes and fears communicate no vibration to the heart; the composition refers us only to the writer; we pronounce the name of *Cato* but we think on Addison.[23]

The Drummer

The Drummer is one of those plays that seems to make little impression on many readers because it is neither very bad nor very good. It was several times revived but never ran long; even the most fervent Addisonians admire its depiction of domestic virtues but find its presentation dull. There is an irony in *The Drummer's* failure to receive either contemporary or subsequent savor. It is simply Addison's most finished play, his best piece of stagecraft. *The Drummer* outdoes *Rosamond* or *Cato* in many ways. It is a more subtle adaptation of a source; it gives a more persuasive portrait of human virtue; it links closely the action of plot and subplot; it adjusts readily to the conventions of its genre; and it offers more interesting stage business. What *The Drummer's* failure illustrates perhaps is that there is more to dramaturgy than a well-made play and that Addison's genius is for something that is not capable of sustained stage presentation.

Act I opens with the three clowns of the play—the butler, the coachman, and the gardener—discussing their fears of a ghost that haunts the estate of Sir George Trueman. The ghost seems to be Sir George himself, killed recently in battle. The one person not afraid of the ghost is Abigail, servant to Sir George's wife.

Abigail knows that the ghost is really Mr. Fantome, a London beau who will pay her a thousand pounds to help him win the widow's hand in marriage. Disguised in Sir George's clothes, wearing a false scar and beating a drum, Fantome hopes to drive off Tinsel, a rival suitor. Lady Trueman ostensibly prefers Tinsel to Fantome, but in fact cares for neither man.

In Act II the real Sir George returns, eager to find out how faithful his wife has been since his rumored death fourteen months before. With the help of Vellum, his steward, Sir George plans to enter the household disguised as a conjuror to witness Lady Trueman's behavior. Vellum is to arrange his admittance, and to learn from Abigail all that goes on in the house.

In Act III Tinsel tries to win Abigail to his side by promising her marriage with a vigorous but poor Horse-Guardsman. Vellum introduces George disguised as a conjuror who immediately ires Tinsel by foretelling the failure of his courtship to Lady Trueman. Meanwhile Vellum has gone to work on Abigail: with liquor, love, and a promise of marriage, he tries to win her confidence.

In Act IV Abigail reveals to Vellum the secret of Fantome hidden in the walls—disguise, drum, and all. Determined that she will keep the money she has collected, Vellum helps her coach Fantome. He teaches him witty love-making while he exposes Tinsel's mercenary interest. Tinsel's last interview with the widow is interrupted by the appearance of Fantome as Sir George's ghost; the frightened suitor skips off the stage in rhythm with the beating drum.

Now that Tinsel is gone and only Fantome remains to be routed, Sir George plans a ghostly visitation of his own in Act V. First, in his role as conjuror, he tests his wife's fondness for her deceased husband by describing for her the events of the wedding day and wedding night; he finds her suitably moved by the memories recalled. She further eases his mind by confessing her dislike for Tinsel. Reassured Sir George routs Fantome when, both dressed as ghosts, they meet face to face. Abigail likewise flees when she recognizes her master. After Sir George reveals himself to his deserving and surprised wife, they look to a comfortable and revived life together. Sir George display his magnanimity to Abigail and Vellum by giving them the thousand pounds Abigail would have received from Fantome.

As the plot summary may have hinted, *The Drummer* draws its story from the last books of Homer's *Odyssey*. Lady Trueman is the modern Penelope, besieged by suitors who crave her fortune but still in love with an absent husband; she uses her wit as Penelope used her weaving to postpone a decision. Sir George is Odysseus, presumed lost in a foreign war, but now returned home in disguise. Vellum is the faithful swineherd to whom the returning master reveals his identity and who helps reclaim the master's rightful place. Tinsel and Fantome are the obnoxious suitors who have literally attempted to make the house their own (Tinsel demands to see Lady Trueman's account books even before he gains her estate and Fantome has taken up residence, albeit behind the wall). The setting recalls the house of Odysseus as well: in the play the suitors and the servants at Trueman Hall eat and drink constantly. In fact, little happens that is not accompanied by a bottle or a carafe. The action proceeds as in the *Odyssey*: Sir George is insulted by Tinsel when he appears disguised as the conjuror; Sir George clears out the suitors, scaring away Tinsel and outdueling Fantome in the contest of the drum, which imitates the contest to bend Odysseus' bow. Sir George seals the Odysseus analogy by declaring, at the play's end, "This Drum will I hang up in my great Hall as the Trophy of the Day."

Based on the classical figures of Odysseus and Penelope, Sir George and Lady Trueman represent marital fidelity conventional in sentimental comedy. In their first stage appearances, the separated lovers do not seem very affectionate. In Act I, Lady Trueman flirts openly with Tinsel, and at the start of Act II the skeptical Sir George learns the details of his Lady's mourning: "Three days, say'st thou? Three whole Days? I'm afraid thou flatterest me!—O Woman! Woman! . . . I find she grieved with a great deal of Good-Breeding." But we soon learn that the lady's lightheartedness and the husband's skepticism are surface only. In each breast beats a sentimental heart. Alone, Lady Trueman describes her real feelings:

I have now been a Widow but fourteen Months, and have had twice
as many Lovers, all of 'em profest Admirers of my Person, but pas-
sionately in love with my Jointure. I think it is a Revenge I owe my
Sex to make an Example of this worthless Tribe of Fellows. . . . I
hope the Diversion I give myself with him is unblameable. I'm sure
'tis necessary to turn my Thoughts off from the Memory of that dear
Man, who has been the greatest Happiness and Affliction of my Life.
(II. i.)

Similarly, upon George's first sight of his lady, he is angry at
the suitors, not at her: "That dear Woman! The Sight of her
unmans me. I cou'd weep for Tenderness, did I not, at the same
time, feel an Indignation rise in me, to see that Wretch with
her" (III. i. 457).

The love plot of *The Drummer* reflects the Addison of the *Spectator* rather than the Addison of *Rosamond* and *Cato*. George and
Lady Trueman are prudent lovers who inhabit a common-sense
middle ground between the passionate adultery of Henry and
Rosamond and the exaggerated abnegation of Portius and Lucia.
The prudent morality of this couple means marital fidelity and
domestic contentment. A hierarchy of characters display the al-
ternatives: the enduring love of Sir George and Lady Trueman,
the unpassionate but honest affection of Vellum and Abigail, the
dishonest affection of Fantome and Tinsel for the widow's
jointure.

The other themes of *The Drummer* likewise advocate the prudential values of the *Spectator* and are dramatized by a hierarchy
of characters. At issue are the possible existence of a spirit world
and the proper conduct of an estate. The prudent philosophy is
a reasonable respect for the possibility of a supernatural world
from which Sir George's ghost is supposedly arisen.[24] The servants
superstitiously accept the reality of the ghost; Tinsel is foolishly
skeptical of any belief; in the middle is the cautious attitude of
the Truemans who know that ghosts may be frauds but who do
not dismiss the possibility of a spiritual world. The prudential
estate economy is shown in Sir George's knowing balance of thrift
and largess; it stands between Vellum's bookkeeping mentality
and Tinsel's ruinous luxury.

Most of the comedy in the play centers around the servant characters. Occasionally Addison raises a laugh by playing upon their stereotypical stupidity. When Sir George is disguised as a conjuror, the butler, the coachman, and the gardener are too scared to remain in his presence; all three have to rush out together to fetch a pen and a piece of paper. When Sir George proceeds to tell their fortunes, each is awestruck. For instance,

Gardener.	The Butler and I, Mr. Doctor, were both of us in Love at the same time with a certain Person.
Sir George.	A Woman.
Gardener.	How cou'd he know that? [Aside] (V. i.)

But more interestingly several servants have a sense of snobbish self-importance that is a delightful mirror of their betters' attitudes. The coachman, for instance, reacts to the coming of the ghostly drummer by declaring, "I'll give Madam warning, that's flat—I've always liv'd in Sober Families. I'll not disparage my self to be a Servant in a House that is haunted." Similarly, Abigail justifies to her employer the extraordinary fee of a thousand pounds for her help in winning Lady Trueman's hand in marriage: "Why, truly now Mr. *Fantome,* I shou'd think myself a very bad Woman, if I had done what I do, for a Farthing less."

But the comic achievement of the play is Vellum, Sir George's steward. Vellum illustrates one of the significant trends in sentimental comedy: the hero's confidant is no longer a fellow rake but a humorous and kindly servant. Vellum is a humours character; he always displays the steward's mentality no matter what the subject. He always itemizes and lists. For example, when he receives a note from the supposedly dead Sir George, he reacts:

This amazeth me! and yet the Reasons why I should believe he is still living are manifold—First, Because this has often been the Case with other Military Adventurers.

Secondly, Because the News of his Death was first published in *Dier's Letter.*

Thirdly, Because this Letter can be written by none but himself—I know his Hand and the manner of Spelling.

Fourthly. . . . (II. i.)

Besides itemizing and listing, Vellum always tries to behave
seriously as becomes the dignity of his position. When he cannot
restrain his sense of humor, he apologizes, "You will pardon me
for being jocular." Addison plays this humours characteristic off
against the emotions of other characters. And Vellum's account-
book mentality on occasion drives Sir George, eager to discover
the situation at the house, to distraction. In Act III Vellum
returns from a mission to Lady Trueman:

Sir George.	Well *Vellum,* I'm impatient to hear your Success.
Vellum.	First, let me lock the Door.
Sir George.	Will your Lady admit me?
Vellum.	If this Lock is not mended soon, it will be quite spoiled.
Sir George.	Prithee let the Lock alone at present, and answer me.
Vellum.	Delays in Business are dangerous—I must send for the Smith next Week—and in the mean time will take a minute of it.
Sir George.	But what says your Lady?
Vellum.	This Pen is naught, and wants mending—My Lady, did you say? (III. i.)

Vellum, however, grows in the play into more than the portrait
of an eccentric mentality. He is witty enough to use his itemizing
habit and usual apology with devastating results against Tinsel.
When Tinsel asks Vellum for a loan of money from the estate,
Vellum responds typically, "I will offer you two Reasons for it
. . . First because the Tenement is not in your Disposal; and
Secondly, because it will never be in your Disposal; and so fare
you well, good *Mr. Tinsel.* Ha, ha, ha! You will pardon me for
being jocular." Of course, there is no pardon—and no recourse—
against Vellum's triumph.

Vellum is also a delightful lover, as his wooing of Abigail (Act
III, scene i) demonstrates. He is the master of the jargon of love
as well as of the jargon of stewardship.

Vellum.	This Middle Finger, Mrs. *Abigal,* has a pretty Neighbour—A Wedding Ring would become it mightily—He, he, he.
Abigail.	You're so full of your Jokes. Ay, but where must I find one for it?
Vellum.	I design this Thimble only as the Forerunner of it, they will set off each other, and are—indeed a twofold Emblem. The first will put you in mind of being a good Huswife, and the other of being a good Wife. Ha, ha, ha!
Abigail.	Yes, yes, I see you laugh at me.
Vellum.	Indeed I am serious.
Abigail.	I thought you had quite forsaken me—I am sure you cannot forget the many repeated Vows and Promises you formerly made me.
Vellum.	I shou'd as soon forget the Multiplication Table. (III. i.)

Despite its construction and good humor, *The Drummer* is not any better than a fair play. There are several reasons; the character of Vellum cannot carry a play in which the leads are mediocre characterizations. Sir George has some life as he intrigues to drum the suitors out of the house, but Lady Trueman displays little wit in her plan to take revenge upon the men. The servants have one good scene and several clever lines, but most scenes and lines are unremarkable. Most importantly the play has all the virtues of the *Spectator,* but these are not dramatic virtues. The *Spectator* did its work on a half-sheet, requiring a few minutes' reading; *The Drummer* runs to scores of pages and requires an evening to read or to attend. The Addisonian virtues of good humor and mild cleverness stand out in an interlude but cannot carry a full performance.

Chapter Nine
Conclusion

Most writers have two reputations. One they gain from literary history, one they gain from readers. Both of Addison's reputations are likely to remain as they are now.

Historically Addison is the quintessential writer of Queen Anne's England. He flourished in several genres characteristic of the period which found few imitators or exploiters in subsequent generations: imitation classical poetry, Latin verse, declamatory tragedy, the dialogue, and sentimental comedy. The only genre which had great influence and in which Addison was specially skilled was periodical journalism.

With Steele, Addison shares the credit for a new literary form that mated journalism with art. The *Tatler* and the *Spectator* spawned a respectable progeny of periodicals in the eighteenth and nineteenth centuries, raised the essay to literary dignity, and made fit subject matter out of the daily life and domestic concerns which became the stuff of the novel. With Swift, Addison shares the credit for refining English prose into a medium that at once equaled poetry and supplanted it as a mode in which to express philosophy, history, and criticism. Addison's style had another effect: English-speaking generations literally went to school for his "sweet Vergilian prose." Ben Franklin was only one of many who incorporated Addison's essays into the school curriculum as a model for students.[1] Franklin himself, as well as Thomas Hardy and others, heeded Johnson's advise to give their days and nights to Addison in pursuit of the middle style.

Addison's essays, for better or worse, educated a civilization. Victorian Englishmen especially looked upon him as the man who rescued literature and society from the degeneracy of the Restoration court on one hand and the fanaticism of Puritanism on the other.² Addison's essays promoting rational belief, tasteful judgments in the arts, and acceptance of social hierarchy became the sugar that Sunday-school lessons were made of; indeed his essays were anthologized into such texts. But if today we are not as impressed as people were in the nineteenth century with Addison's role in founding bourgeois society, it is nonetheless hard to deny him respect for contributing substantially to English civilization. Whatever "civilization" may mean, its definition includes the notion that individuals and a society as a whole possess a willingness to accept diversity and to forego aggression against those who disagree; Addison's promotion of both the best of classical culture and the best of modern thinking helped England to a rational and secular civilization more stable and less violent in the eighteenth century than in the seventeenth.³

Addison's place in literary history, then, is firm but modest. That seems to leave him in the hands of the critics rather than of readers. As James Sutherland remarked, "If Addison is a writer in no immediate danger of being forgotten, he is one that is not very actively remembered."⁴ Though not perhaps as actively as other authors, Addison is yet remembered in his own way.

"Faint" is a favorite word for Addison among those who do not actively remember him. Indeed one cannot sit down and read his works at length with satisfaction. Shakespeare draws the reader increasingly into the poetry of his language and his vision of life; Samuel Johnson draws the reader increasingly into the complexity of individual consciousness; Addison, however, pleases in small but repeated doses. But he unfailingly pleases. The careful prose and comfortable pace do not disappoint upon rereading. Even his poems and plays give pleasure most when they are read like his periodical pieces: a quarter of an hour's attention every once in a while. Like Bishop Hurd, most enjoyers of Addison come to the "full value of his writings" after renewed visits.⁵

Like his style Addison's worldview is not for all seasons. He pays little attention to the heights and depths, passions and despair of human life. Instead he pokes fun at silly fashions or "bad" taste in the arts or selfish opinions. His satire, unlike Swift's, hardly takes one to the heart of the matter. But neither is Addison's concern out of date or irrelevant. Fads in dress and thinking rapidly change, but the human disposition to faddishness remains. Beaux and belles give way to flappers and flowerchildren; virtuosos and projectors metamorphose into entrepreneurs. Elitism and oddity often masquerade as excellence, and any ally of the latter helps penetrate the ever-changing disguises of the former. Addison may not pay attention to many things, but he never ignores what deserves praise within his own sphere. "The Addisonian world is not one to live in at all times, but it is a good one to fall back into when the day's work is over and a man's feet on the fender and his pipe in his mouth. Good sense is no substitute for Reason; but as a rest from Reason it has distinct advantages over Jargon."[6]

Notes and References

The best modern edition of Addison is the two-volume set *The Miscellaneous Works of Joseph Addison,* edited by A. C. Guthkelch (London: George Bell, 1914). It contains all works except the periodical essays. The first volume contains the plays and poems, the second the prose works. To simplify annotation, all references to Addison's works are to this edition unless otherwise cited. I cite parenthetically line numbers for the poems, act-scene-line numbers for the plays, and page numbers for the prose works.

Chapter One

1. Gerald M. and Lois O. Straka, *A Certainty in Succession,* Borzoi History of England, Volume 4: 1640–1815 (New York: Alfred A. Knopf, 1973), p. 76.

2. J. H. Plumb, *The Growth of Political Stability in England 1675–1725* (New York: Macmillan, 1967), pp. 52–53, 136–137.

3. James William Johnson, *The Formation of Neoclassical Thought* (Princeton: Princeton University Press, 1967), p. 68.

4. Cf. J. W. Saunders, *The Profession of English Letters* (London: Routledge and Kegan Paul, 1964), pp. 94–97.

5. "Nova Philosophia Veteri Praeferenda Est," trans. by Richard Rawlinson, *The Works of Joseph Addison,* with notes by Richard Hurd and edited by Henry G. Bohn (London, 1899), 6:612.

6. John Richard Green, Introduction to *The Essays of Joseph Addison* (London: Roger de Coverley Club, n.d.), p. ix.

7. Peter Smithers, *The Life of Joseph Addison* (Oxford, 1968), p. 29.

8. Pat Rogers, *The Augustan Vision* (New York: Barnes and Noble, 1974), pp. 81–83.

9. Ragnhild Hatton, *Europe in the Age of Louis XIV* (New York: Harcourt Brace and World, 1969), pp. 27–30.

10. Preface, *The Works of Joseph Addison,* 1:iv.

11. Joseph Warton, *An Essay on the Genius and Writing of Pope* (London: W. J. Robertson, 1806), 1:29.

12. Samuel Johnson, "Life of Addison," *Lives of the English Poets* (London, 1925), 1:368.

Chapter Two

1. The translation by Christopher Hayes is in *The Works of Joseph Addison,* 6:589.

2. The translation by Thomas Newcombe is in *The Works of Joseph Addison,* 6:579.

3. The translation by Thomas Newcombe is in *The Works of Joseph Addison,* 6:585.

4. Leicester Bradner, *Musae Anglicanae: A History of Anglo-Latin Poetry 1500–1925* (New York: Modern Language Association of America, 1940), p. 210.

5. Quoted in *The Works of Joseph Addison,* 6:573.

6. The translation is in *The Works of Joseph Addison,* 6:575.

7. The translation by George Sewell is in *The Works of Joseph Addison,* 6:557.

8. The translation by Nicholas Amhurst is in *The Works of Joseph Addison,* 6:577.

9. Richmond P. Bond, *English Burlesque Poetry* (1932; rpt. New York: Russell and Russell, 1964), p. 215.

10. The translation by Thomas Newcombe is in *The Works of Joseph Addison,* 6:560.

11. Ibid., p. 563.

12. The translation by Thomas Newcombe is in *The Works of Joseph Addison,* 6:555.

Chapter Three

1. See Lillian D. Bloom, "Addison as Translator: A Problem in Neoclassical Scholarship," *Studies in Philology* 46 (1949): 31–53, for a thorough discussion of Addison's methods.

2. James E. Philips, "Poetry and Music in the Seventeenth Century," *Studies and Georgian Moments,* ed. Earl Miner (Berkeley and Los Angeles: University of California Press, 1972), p. 5.

3. Giles Jacob, *An Historical Account of the Lives and Writings of Our Most Considerable English Poets* (London: Edward Curll, 1720), 2:247.

4. Smithers, p. 24.

5. William Bowman Piper, *The Heroic Couplet* (Cleveland and London: Case Western Reserve University Press, 1969), p. 364.

6. *The Works of Joseph Addison,* 1:230, n. 2.

7. Michael Foss, *The Age of Patronage: The Arts in England 1660–1750* (Ithaca: Cornell University Press, 1971), p. 145.

8. Not untypical is the assessment of Correlli Barnett, *The First Churchill* (New York: Putnam, 1974), p. 122.

9. Warton, 1:29.

10. Piper, p. 365.

11. Quoted by Robert D. Horn, *Marlborough: A Survey* (New York: Garland Publishers, 1975), p. 78.

12. Henry L. Snyder, ed., *The Marlborough-Godolphin Correspondence* (Oxford: Clarendon Press, 1975), 1:344.

13. Horn, p. 85.

Chapter Four

1. Lucy Aikin, *The Life of Joseph Addison* (London: Longman, 1843), 1:98.

2. Horace Walpole, *The Letters of Horace Walpole,* ed. Paget Toynbee (Oxford: Clarendon Press, 1903–1905), 1:60.

3. Johnson, 1:331.

4. See also Donald R. Johnson, "Addison in Italy," *Modern Language Studies* 6 (1976):32–36.

5. *A Table of the principal matters contained in Mr. Addison's Remarks on Several Parts of Italy, etc. in the Years 1701, 1702, 1703* (London: n.p., 1705), pp. 1–3.

6. Smithers, p. 53.

7. Joseph Addison, *Letters of Joseph Addison,* ed. Walter Graham (Oxford, 1941), p. 29.

8. Bonamy Dobrée, *English Literature in the Early Eighteenth Century* (London: Oxford University Press, 1959), p. 120.

9. Addison, *Letters,* p. 35.

10. Richard Hurd, "On the Manner of Writing Dialogues," *The Works of Richard Hurd D.D.* (London: T. Cadell and W. Davies, 1811), 3:22.

11. Elizabeth Merrill, *The Dialogue in English Literature,* Yale Studies in English 42 (New Haven: Yale University Press, 1911), p. 68.

12. Snyder, 1:322, n.2.

13. William A. Shaw, ed., *Calendar of Treasury Books* (London: Her Majesty's Stationery Office, 1938), 19 (January 1704 to March 1705): 535.

14. *The Works of Joseph Addison,* 4:169.

15. Quoted by G. M. Trevelyan, *England Under Queen Anne: Ramillies and the Union with Scotland* (London: Longmans, Green, and Co., 1932), p. 325.

16. *Examiner* 1 (Thursday, August 3, 1710), p. 1.

17. *The Works of Joseph Addison,* 4:376. The "Letter" is reprinted in *The Prose Works of Jonathan Swift,* ed. Herbert Davis (Oxford: Basil Blackwell, 1940), 3:221–27.

18. *The Works of Joseph Addison,* 4:385–86.

19. Ibid., 4:386.

20. Ibid.

21. John Gay, *The Present State of Wit in a Letter to a Friend in the Country* (1711), Augustan Reprint Society Publication 3 (Los Angeles: William Andrews Clark Memorial Library, 1947), p. 2.

22. Bertrand A. Goldgar, *The Curse of Party: Swift's Relations with Addison and Steele* (Lincoln: University of Nebraska Press, 1961), p. 121.

Chapter Five

1. Richard Steele, "Dedication to *The Drummer,*" *The Works of Joseph Addison,* 5:148.

2. Bickerstaff's history is related in Richmond P. Bond, "Isaac Bickerstaff, Esq.," *Restoration and 18th Century Literature: Essays in Honor of Alan Dugald McKillop* (Chicago: University of Chicago Press, 1963), pp. 103–24.

3. Lewis Gibbs, ed., *The Tatler* (London: J. M. Dent and Sons, 1953), p. 1. No complete modern edition of the *Tatler* exists, but numerous old editions or selections are available. Most of the issues identified as Addison's are in the second volume of *The Works of Joseph Addison.* For Addison's essays I recommend this edition, and for Steele the Gibbs volume. For the convenience of those who have other editions of the *Tatler,* my text cites only the number of the issue in which a quotation appears.

4. F. W. Bateson, "Addison, Steele, and the Periodical Essay," *History of Literature in the English Language,* ed. Roger Lonsdale (London, 1971), 4:156.

5. For an analysis of Steele's innovation, see Walter Graham, *English Literary Periodicals* (New York, 1930), pp. 65–66.

6. Henry Troyer, *Ned Ward of Grub Street* (Cambridge, Mass.: Harvard University Press, 1946), p. 167.

7. Richard Achurch, "Richard Steele, Gazetteer and Bickerstaff," *Studies in the Early English Periodical*, ed. Richmond P. Bond (Chapel Hill: University of North Carolina Press, 1957), p. 67.

8. Richmond P. Bond, *The Tatler: The Making of a Journal* (Cambridge, Mass., 1971), p. 31.

9. Graham, p. 90.

10. Gay, pp. 10–11.

11. Calhoun Winton, *Captain Steele* (Baltimore: The Johns Hopkins Press, 1964), pp. 93–94.

12. Bond, *The Tatler: The Making of a Journal*, pp. 93–94.

13. Walter Graham, "Addison's Travel Letters in the *Tatler* and *Guardian*," *Philological Quarterly* 15 (1936):99.

14. Steele, "Dedication to *The Drummer*," 5:147.

Chapter Six

1. W. J. Bate and Albrecht Strauss, eds., *The Rambler*, The Yale Edition of the Works of Samuel Johnson (New Haven: Yale University Press, 1969), 3:129.

2. Gay, p. 6.

3. Donald F. Bond, Introduction to *The Spectator* (Oxford: Clarendon Press, 1965), 1:xlv.

4. *The Spectator*, 1:6. All subsequent references are from this edition and are identified by issue number in the text. From *The Spectator* edited by Donald F. Bond (5 volumes), ©1965 Oxford University Press. Reprinted by permission of Oxford University Press.

5. Gay, p. 6.

6. Donald F. Bond, 1:lix.

7. Bateson, 4:151.

8. Ibid., 4:159.

9. Edward Pitcher, "On the Conventions of Eighteenth-Century British Short Fiction," *Studies in Short Fiction* 12 (1975):201.

10. James George Frazier, "Sir Roger de Coverley," *Sir Roger de Coverley and Other Literary Pieces* (London: Macmillan and Company, 1920), pp. 3–61.

11. William Hazlitt, "Lectures on the English Comic Writers," *Complete Works of William Hazlitt* (1931; rpt. New York: AMS Press, 1967), 6:98.

12. Ian Gordon, *The Movement of English Prose* (Bloomington: Indiana University Press, 1966), p. 139.

13. Bateson, 4:148–49.

14. Ronald Paulson, *The Fictions of Satire* (Baltimore: Johns Hopkins University Press, 1967), p. 211.

15. Preface, *The Works of Joseph Addison,* 1:ix. See also Robert D. Chambers, "Addison at Work on the *Spectator*," *Modern Philology* 56 (1959):145–53, for specific instances in which Addison turned a little "hint" into an essay.

16. Lillian D. Bloom, "Addison's Popular Aesthetic: The Rhetoric of the *Paradise Lost* Papers," *The Author in His Work,* ed. Louis L. Martz and Aubrey Williams (New Haven: Yale University Press, 1978), p. 266.

17. Dionysius Longinus, *Dionysius Longinus on the Sublime,* trans. William Smith (London: J. Watts, 1739), p. 16.

18. Ibid., p. 15.

19. T. R. Henn, *Longinus and English Criticism* (Cambridge: Cambridge University Press, 1934), p. 11.

20. For a study of the transition from notes to essay see Albert Furtwangler, "Addison's Editing of the Papers on Imagination," *Wascana Review* 11 (1976):3–19.

21. Kenneth MacLean, *John Locke and English Literature of the 18th Century* (New Haven: Yale University Press, 1936), p. 11.

22. See Clarence DeWitt Thorpe, "Addison and Some of His Predecessors on 'Novelty,' " *PMLA* 52 (1937):1114–29.

23. C. H. Salter, "Dryden and Addison," *Modern Language Review* 69 (1974):34–35.

24. For a schematic, thorough account see John Timmerman, "Divinity and Creativity: The Aesthetic Framework of Joseph Addison," *University of Dayton Review* 8 (1971):17–28.

25. Edward Bliss Reed, "Two Notes on Addison," *Modern Philology* 6 (1908):189.

26. Ralph Lawrence, "The English Hymn," *Essays and Studies* 7 (1954):107.

27. See Donald Kay, *Short Fiction in "The Spectator"* (University: University of Alabama Press, 1975).

28. Paulson, p. 211ff. See also Robert H. Hopkins, " 'The Good Old Cause' in Pope, Addison and Steele," *Review of English Studies* 17 (1966):62–68.

29. Mark Longaker, *English Biography in the 18th Century* (Philadelphia: University of Pennsylvania Press, 1931), p. 84.

30. Walter Raleigh, *The English Novel* (London: J. Murray, 1895), p. 120.

Chapter Seven

1. Walter Graham, *English Literary Periodicals,* p. 82.

2. *The Works of Joseph Addison,* 4:246. Future references to this edition are cited parenthetically by issue number in the text.

3. *The Spectator* (Oxford, 1965), 4:501. Future references from this edition are cited parenthetically by issue number in the text.

4. *The Works of Joseph Addison,* 4:339. Future references from this edition are cited parenthetically by issue number in the text.

5. See Donald McDonald, "The Logic of Addison's Freeholder," *Papers on Language and Literature* 4 (1968):20–34.

6. Johnson, 1:342.

Chapter Eight

1. Steele, "Dedication to *The Drummer,*" 5:152.

2. John Oldmixon, *An Essay of Criticism* (1728), Augustan Reprint Society Publications 107–108 (Los Angeles: William Andrews Clark Memorial Library, 1964), p. 6.

3. Roger Fiske, *English Theatre Music in the Eighteenth Century* (London: Oxford University Press, 1973), p. 46.

4. A. W. Ward, *Dramatic Literature to the Death of Queen Anne* (1899; rpt. New York: Octagon Books, 1966), 3:323, n. 1.

5. Warton, 1:55.

6. Bonamy Dobrée, "The First Victorian," *Essays in Biography* (London, 1925), p. 239.

7. Johnson, 1:354.

8. George Sewell, *A Vindication of the English Stage Exemplified in the CATO of Mr. ADDISON* (London: W. Mears, 1716), p. iv.

9. Voltaire, "English Tragedy," *The Works of Voltaire,* trans. William H. Fleming (New York: The St. Hubert Guild, 1901), 39:50–51.

10. Frederic M. Litto, "Addison's *Cato* in the Colonies," *William and Mary Quarterly* 23 (1966):447.

11. James Broaden, *Memoirs of the Life of John Philip Kemble* (Philadelphia: Robert H. Small, 1825), p. 555.

12. Bonamy Dobrée, *Restoration Tragedy 1660–1720* (Oxford: Clarendon Press, 1929), p. 173.

13. Ward, 3:441.

14. *The Dramatic Censor, or Critical Companion* (London: J. Bell, 1770), 1:459.

15. Mary Wortley Montague, *Essays and Poems and "Simplicity," A Comedy* (Oxford: Clarendon Press, 1977), p. 64.

16. See M. M. Kelsall, "The Meaning of Addison's *Cato,*" *Review of English Studies,* new series, 17 (1966):149–61.

17. Also see the discussion of the papers on tragedy in Chapter 6 above.

18. *Cato Examin'd or, Animadversions on the Fable or Plot, Manners, Sentiments, and Diction of the New Tragedy of "Cato"* (London: J. Pemberton, 1713), p. 17.

19. Oldmixon, p. 7.

20. Michael M. Cohen, "The Imagery of Addison's *Cato* and the Whig Sublime," *CEA Critic* 38 (1976):23–25, and Donald O. Rogers, "Addison's *Cato:* Teaching Through Imagery," *CEA Critic* 36 (1974):17–18, take different but reconcilable positions on the imagery.

21. "Pro Sestio," xxviii, 60, *The Speeches,* trans. R. Gardner (Cambridge, Mass.: Harvard University Press, 1958), p. 115.

22. A good study of Cato's character is James S. Malek, "The Fifth Act of Addison's *Cato,*" *Neuphilologische Mitteilungen* 74 (1973):515–19.

23. Samuel Johnson, "A Preface to Shakespeare," *Johnson on Shakespeare,* ed. Arthur Sherbo, The Yale Edition of the Works of Samuel Johnson (New Haven: Yale University Press, 1968), 7:84.

24. See Donald C. Baker, "Witchcraft, Addison and *The Drummer,*" *Studia Neophilologica* 31 (1950):174–81.

Chapter Nine

1. Ben Franklin, "Idea of the English School," *The Papers of Ben Franklin* (New Haven: Yale University Press, 1961), 4:102–108.

2. Alexandre Beljame, *Men of Letters and the English Public in the Eighteenth Century,* trans. E. O. Lorimer (London: Kegan, Paul, Trench, Trubner and Co., 1948), pp. 306–307.

3. See Peter Gay, "The Spectator as Actor: Addison in Perspective," *Encounter* 29 (1967):32, for an excellent discussion of the civilizing force of Addison's writing.

4. James Sutherland, "The Last Years of Joseph Addison," *Background for Queen Anne* (London, 1939), p. 127.

5. Richard Hurd and William Mason, *Correspondence of Richard Hurd and William Mason,* ed. Ernest Harold Pearce (Cambridge: Cambridge University Press, 1932), p. 76.

6. C. S. Lewis, "Addison," *Eighteenth Century English Literature: Modern Essays in Criticism,* ed. James Clifford (New York: Oxford University Press, 1959), p. 156.

Selected Bibliography

PRIMARY SOURCES

1. Collected Works

The Miscellaneous Works of Joseph Addison. Edited by A. C. Guthkelch.
2 vols. London: George Bell and Sons, 1914. The modern edition
which is currently authoritative for the plays, poems, and non-
periodical prose. It does not include any periodical essays.

The Works of Joseph Addison. Edited by Richard Hurd, collected by
Henry G. Bohn. 6 vols. London: George Bell and Sons, 1854–1856.
The most frequently reprinted and thus most readily available
edition, it contains some miscellaneous material and is especially
valuable for the minor periodical essays, often unavailable else-
where.

2. Collections of Periodical Essays

Addison and Steele: Selections from the Tatler *and the* Spectator. Edited by
Robert J. Allen. New York: Holt, Rinehart & Winston, 1968.
A balanced selection of both authors at their best on a variety of
topics.

Critical Essays from the Spectator *by Joseph Addison.* Edited by Donald
F. Bond. New York: Oxford University Press, 1970. Well annotated and complete collection of *Spectator* essays on literature,
the theater, and aesthetics.

The De Coverley Papers from the Spectator. Edited by O. M. Meyers.
Oxford: Clarendon Press, 1956. The most scholarly of many editions of these perennially popular essays.

The Letters of Joseph Addison. Edited by Walter Graham. Oxford: Clarendon Press, 1941. The standard, more or less complete, edition.

The Spectator. Edited by Donald F. Bond. 5 vols. Oxford: Clarendon
Press, 1965. The definitive edition. Provides the model for future
modern editions of the *Tatler, Guardian, Freeholder,* and other
eighteenth-century periodicals.

SECONDARY SOURCES

1. Bibliographies
Evans, James E., and Wall, John N., Jr. *A Guide to Prose Fiction in the* Tatler *and the* Spectator. New York: Garland Publishers, 1977. An indispensable guide providing a summary of each *Tatler* and *Spectator* and an annotated bibliography on the fiction in these periodicals.

Rogal, Samuel J. "Joseph Addison (1672–1719): A Checklist of Works and Major Scholarship" *Bulletin of the New York Public Library* 77 (1974):236–250. Although not as inclusive as the *New Cambridge Bibliography* on original works, Rogal's is much easier to use because entries are classified according to genre. The criticism is listed under each of Addison's works; some items are not listed in the *NCBEL.*

Watson, George, ed. *New Cambridge Bibliography of English Literature.* Cambridge: Cambridge University Press, 1971. 2:1098–1112. The most complete bibliography but not entirely satisfactory: much important Addison criticism is contained in articles and books on larger topics which are too general for listing here.

2. Biographies
Addisoniana. 2 vols. London: R. Philips, 1803. A collection of anecdotes and passages from eighteenth-century writers about the personality and works of Addison; also selections from Addison's letters.

Dobrée, Bonamy. "The First Victorian." In *Essays in Biography: 1680–1726.* Oxford: Oxford University Press, 1925. The first modern biography of Addison, Dobrée's account is lively and prejudiced. As the title suggests, Dobrée finds Addison a cynosure of the worst Victorian attitudes: self-centered, smug about the world, content with bourgeois values.

Goldgar, Bertrand A. *The Curse of Party: Swift's Relation with Addison and Steele.* Lincoln: University of Nebraska Press, 1961. Although predominantly about Swift, it presents a fascinating close-up of the world of party writers in the reign of Queen Anne.

Smithers, Peter. *The Life of Joseph Addison.* Oxford: Clarendon Press, 1968. The most detailed and sympathetic—in short, the best—

biography to date, although it gives little attention to analysis of the literary works.

Spence, Joseph. *Observations, Anecdotes, and Characters of Books and Men.* Edited by James M. Osborne. 2 vols. Oxford: Clarendon Press, 1966. Contains anecdotes about Addison, especially by Pope; good notes help distinguish reliable from unreliable comments.

Sutherland, James. "The Last Years of Joseph Addison." In *Background for Queen Anne.* London: Methuen, 1939. Pp. 127–44. Like Dobrée, Sutherland stresses the negative side of Addison's character, especially attributing to him a tendency to pose as the epitome of the well-balanced eighteenth-century Christian.

Tyers, Thomas. *An Historical Essay on Mr. Addison.* 1783; rpt. New York: Garland Publishing, 1977. A rare, lively, unjustly ignored portrait of Addison which stresses him as a man of wit.

3. Critical Studies

Bateson, F. W. "Addison, Steele and the Periodical Essay." In *History of Literature in the English Language.* Edited by Roger Lonsdale. London: Barrie and Jenkins, 1971. 4:144–64. A brief and lucid summing up of Addison's place in English literary history.

Beljame, Alexandre. "Joseph Addison." In *Men of Letters and the English Public in the Eighteenth Century.* Translated by E. O. Lorimer. London: Kegan, Paul, Trench, Trubner and Co., 1948. Pp. 212–317. The classical formulation of the adulatory view of Addison as a reformer of manners and bearer of Enlightened civilization.

Bloom, Edward A. and Lillian D. *Joseph Addison's Sociable Animal: In the Market Place, On the Hustings, In the Pulpit.* Providence: Brown University Press, 1971. An ambitious synthesis of Addison's thoughts on society, economics, and religion.

Bloom, Lillian D. "Addison as Translator: A Problem in Neoclassical Scholarship." *Studies in Philology* 46 (1949):31–53. The major statement on a neglected part of Addison's literary corpus.

Bond, Richard P. *The Tatler: The Making of a Journal.* Cambridge, Mass.: Harvard University Press, 1971. A fascinating study of how Steele and Addison put together their first joint periodical. It treats every aspect from writing to printing to distribution.

Chambers, Robert D. "Addison at Work on the *Spectator.*" *Modern Philology* 56 (1959):145–53. An interesting study which shows how Addison crafted finished *Spectator* essays out of "many pieces, that had lain by him in little hints and minutes."

Elioseff, Lee Andrew. *The Cultural Milieu of Addison's Literary Criticism.* Austin: University of Texas Press, 1963. Although in a later article the author has repudiated some of the book's assumptions and conclusions, it remains the most comprehensive view of Addison's criticism.

Gay, Peter. "The Spectator as Actor: Addison in Perspective." *Encounter* 29 (1967):27–32. A modern evaluation of Beljame's view of Addison as a shaper of English manners and customs in an otherwise brutal age.

Graham, Walter. *English Literary Periodicals.* New York: Thomas Nelson and Sons, 1930. The first three chapters offer a lucid discussion of the ancestors, contemporaries, and descendants of the *Tatler* and *Spectator.*

Hansen, David A. "Addison on Ornament and Style," *Studies in Criticism and Aesthetics, 1660–1800: Essays in Honor of Samuel Holt Monk.* Minneapolis: University of Minnesota Press, 1967. Pp. 94–127. One of the few articles which looks at Addison's criticism in both the periodical essays and earlier works.

Horn, Robert D. "Addison's 'Campaign' and Macaulay." *PMLA* 53 (1948):886–902. Probably the most accurate account of the poem crucial to the beginning of Addison's political career.

Humphreys, A. R. "Steele, Addison and Their Periodical Essays." British Council Pamphlet, 1959. The best short study of the background format and techniques of literature's most famous team.

Johnson, Samuel. "Life of Addison." In *Lives of the English Poets.* London: J. M. Dent, 1925. I:327–368. All students of Addison start with Johnson's assessment of both the man and his works.

Kay, Donald. *Short Fiction in the Spectator.* University, Ala.: University of Alabama Press, 1975. The best and most comprehensive study of fictional techniques used by Addison and Steele.

Kelsall, M. M. "The Meaning of Addison's *Cato.*" *Review of English Studies* 17 (1966):149–61. One of the first and most perceptive readings of the play to get beyond and behind the political reputation.

Lannering, Jan. *Studies in the Prose Style of Joseph Addison.* Essays and Studies on English Language and Literature 9. Cambridge, Mass.: Harvard University Press, 1951. A highly technical discussion of style, but with many perceptive comments on the eighteenth-century background of prose style.

Lewis, C. S. "Addison." In *Eighteenth Century English Literature: Modern Essays in Criticism.* Edited by James Clifford. New York: Oxford University Press, 1959. Pp. 144–57. An important essay stating the case for reading Addison today, despite the accuracy of the Dobrée-Sutherland case for his Victorianism.

Paulson, Ronald. *The Fictions of Satire.* Baltimore: Johns Hopkins Press, 1967. The concluding chapter (210 ff.) has an excellent discussion of Addison and Steele's satiric technique in the *Spectator* papers.

Rogal, Samuel J. "Addison's Spectator Hymns." *NEMLA Newsletter* 2 (1970):8–13. To date, the fullest discussion of the five divine poems.

Thorpe, Clarence DeWitt. "Addison's Contribution to Criticism." *The Seventeenth Century: Studies by R. F. Jones and Others.* Stanford: Standord University Press, 1951. A balanced assessment of Addison's critical achievement.

———. "Addison's Theory of Imagination as Perceptive Response." *Papers of the Michigan Academy of Arts and Sciences* 21 (1936):509–30. One of the best readings of the "Pleasures of the Imagination" essays.

Tuveson, Ernest Lee. *The Imagination as a Means of Grace.* Berkeley and Los Angeles: University of California Press, 1960. Addison's pleasures of the imagination series in the *Spectator* is seen as crucial in the development of romantic aesthetics.

Index